NOTHING ABOUT HEAVEN

Jason Bright

Grosvenor House
Publishing Limited

The right of Jason Bright to be identified as the author of this
work has been asserted by him in accordance with Section 78
of the Copyright, Designs and Patents Act 1988

The book cover picture is copyright to Jason Bright

This book is published by
Grosvenor House Publishing Ltd
28-30 High Street, Guildford, Surrey, GU1 3EL.
www.grosvenorhousepublishing.co.uk

A CIP record for this book
is available from the British Library

ISBN 978-1-78148-386-2

Imagine that someone tells you that when you put blue and yellow together this makes green, and you

Did not know or believe this to be true! Then you are handed a diary which inside has the formula of how to mix blue and yellow together, you follow the formula and actually get green, then what?

Acknowledgements

I WISH TO DEDICATE AN UNDYING GRATITUDE TO SAM AND JO (TRANSCRIPTION CITY) FOR ALL THIER SUPPORT OF WHICH THIS DIARY COULD NEVER HAVE COME TO FRUITION.....

Greece is beautiful, also the people, (Greeks) take some getting used to, you see they don't come to you, you have to go to them, but cigar, cigar (slowly, slowly). It seems to me that if you are a tourist they don't respect you very much. I suppose that's because they have misbehaved in some way so they no longer trust them. But if you are a resident then you may earn respect.

The Greek unlike Turks do not smile at you for long because they don't really have the confidence to do so. But if you work on them over a period of time (or you stay long enough) then they will. The women are not for anyone but the Greeks in fact the women are.

Told by their parents not to smile or socialise with tourists. And if you were lucky enough to go out and try it you would have to be a resident, then there would probably be a shot gun wedding.

I am up in the mountains with a very wide view.
Alas my mind has broadened in to some being new.
Lion Mountains guards me as well as stone gods.
What a beautiful land it makes all the odds.
My mind will travel for and my spirit within.
I shall crawl out of lies and out of sin.

The morning hours here are from 8 till 1 o'clock so they do five hours in the day and then usually sleep it off in the afternoon. Also at 5 to 6 they mostly do another three hours but that's standard. So I only sleep some afternoons. I try not to because it's not really me at the moment but I may soon get into a regular habit but I doubt it.

Everything will work out for me. London England will not be my destiny unless Stella calls in the wind for me. Then to go back will be easy.

In this life all people must have it hard before they have it easy. That is of course if one can learn by their own mistakes.

I went to the top of the mountains where I'm living. What do you think it was like? The view took my breath away. I can see almost the whole of Greece (well not quite) but it seems like it. My faithful 50CC took me all the way here and back.

From the view I could see all around, imagine a birds sight of which the bird takes for granted, well one day we might.

To catch a flight into panoramic
what sense what organic.
I've seen view many times, oh yes.
But the one that I saw makes all others an eye sore.

Tonight I witnesses content! It lays in the stars. What a cluster I saw so many stars of all different lights. I saw the great plough and we saw the great plough and w (the queen) together... as if it were forever. Any people who dates think that there is no other. Life is our huge universe we need not be alive and for the first time I saw the moon through binoculars. I will leave rest to you.

I'm under the stars always and maybe the shapes the way of life. They make up shapes our destiny our life. I've taken all for granted and not seen the stars glory.

Riding a bike is fantastic especially when you don't have to wear a fucking helmet. What a sense of freedom. It's really great, yeah. I have a little motor bike which can go up or down anywhere because the bike is small, is tough though. I hope soon to go to Porous on it and who knows.

A ride on a bike
what an amusement
up up and away, away from the basement.
Awesome machine, that's what it is.
A wondering traveller will use it for this.

Stop a child from being its true self and you have Ha Ha Ha. Stop a day or try to change the stars pattern from its true self then you have Ha Ha Ha. I have noticed that colour does not exist in the night. It vanishes leaving behind only darkness. All also find that the night stops sound from travelling, but that's only I find.

When people want perfection they will only find chaos. For this is because, because is all as it comes and perfection shall prevail. But build strong walls and be not frail.

I'm trying, no that's a lie. I want to give up smoking. There will be a time though when I will have no more.

Don't be over zealous one man told, this is because of their politics bollocks. I bring a bit of common friendliness, it's just what I've heard even if it is over zealous. I went today swimming. Beautiful. I hired a boat and went rowing with a friend, it was very relaxing.

Come swimming with me
in the sea, and I'll show you the glory of the waves
It's so refreshing, a lift up, it can make you a slave.

Page 9 = the bike ride with Bob was fine we both enjoyed the ride and our swim. £10,000 a year I'll need to move on next year, 1992 because I don't think I'm ever going to go back so I had to earn and save to help support me in another country if I don't get work straight away.

I am first wondering of future and past but I shall not think of any of these. What has been has been so what is to come shall come.

I am learning the language little by little: the goal, to be earning money in another country.

The more I learn about myself, the more I'll understand of others.

Who will be my guider?

Who will bring me up or down?

Who will understand me?

That I'm going around and round!!

Fuck "" "" ""

Tonight I saw a film under the stars. What an experience. And I went there, up in the mountains in a modest bike with two other people. So there was three of us. It was lit only by the light of stars for the mountain road as here was no lights. What a trek. I also saw three shooting stars; yeah, three! Wow, how about that then!

The stars that guide me make sure I'm safe.
I'll arrive here safely in my place.
No fear I shall feel for I have faith.
And in my soul I shall have grace.

Well, who knows the money will grow and off I go.

There's a lot I have to go through even here. I will prevail over any problems because I plan on being at peace with myself. If I seek to learn too much too quickly then this could destroy me, so I must move with stealth.

The road is long, but the end is near.
I shall learn. It's quite clear.
Of people and madness, love and sadness.
I shall learn that. I shall be clear.

To enable me to stay away from England I must work. I have five hundred pounds only and if I stay here and work and just get pocket money, then this is all for change.

To be is to be and this is sacred although life in soul may continue after death.

I have always been in the middle of the road and I intend to stay there. I will not be left or right. Who is right? Who is wrong? Well the saga goes on trying to work it out, but let me tell you something.

In the beginning there was water but I'm sure it will end in fire. Who knows if I am truthful or who knows if I'm a liar

The aim is not to use your everyday brain do with instinct. Thought is a diversion from a lot of true actions and feelings. The simple minded of this world (ignorance is bliss) are blessed by god in life in which case it's folly to be wise.

I will play the part of a fool.
When trouble that does not concern me comes,

I will stay with myself and stay as one.
If I were to indulge or have the burdens of the world on my shoulders then I would become very cold.

Well, what do you expect living in this country is re birth to grow up in other areas of life. I can handle it because I live life's little challenges.

After all where would we be without a little and, I mean just a little bit of zest.

I shall come a long way towards understanding of my fellow man.
I know I must be good and graceful as I can.
I shall dismiss stupid thoughts and I shall clear my mind.
This one day may catch on to man kind

I'm going to be alright because I can bend in different directions whilst staying in the middle of the road. It's hard but when assumed, it's easy.

I don't know, neither do I want to know what will come to be.
I shall not try. I shall not try to see then I will be easy.

Hypocrites and lunatics; I'd rather be with lunatics. I'm now just beginning to really understand the Greek way of life, they are in fact very laid back people and they just simply have their ways like everybody else. I know that I will fit in very well with and become part of it if I'm able to stay long enough.

A spit in the ocean is all, but after, it lasts forever. So I have no time to be fine or be clever. Peace is all I shall seek with my unsure voice. I must take this road. I shall go by choice.

Today I had some ideas, but I must just let things ride with the wind, as they should do. The time was pleasurable today, it's being with nature that makes it so delicious. I had a nice omelette and salad which was great.

I want to be me. I like being me. I shall be no one else. I shall come to my own decisions, make my own way through life. If I follow some other body then may the gods protect me, or else.

Well, even if Martians can do work for us ten to the thousand more than us and make life easier it is wrong for them to be slaves for us. Anyway, I have to have more faith in my bike friend he drives so well in the dark. So I must go to another island to see what's going on.

The world is my home, I live in it. I can go where I want, I live in it. The world is my home so here I go. I can live in a hot country or fields with snow. I can go anywhere, you know.

I do not actually like working alone. I prefer to work with people, then it's more fun but no matter. Today I got two lovely letters from 2 friends the letters brought very emotional tears to my eyes. It was very graceful.

It was just what it was and that they were meant to be. The donkey, the goat's cats and dogs were put here together with the sea. It's all part of the great creations, the explosion of life the everything moves and breathes.

It's nice to keep the old, old, but every now and then it's nice to put a sparkle on it. I do till love a game of chess. My Greek is becoming better and soon I will know a lot of it.

My heart I will try to keep joyful like a little child.
I would like to always have good thoughts but nothing too wild.
I want the rather I need the best feelings out of life.

But sometimes it's hard to feel any good or content, but when I do
its right.

We took a ride today. It was a laugh when we took a boat out and
I tried to fly it. You should have seen us. It was a right good giggle.
There is more to do around the house and it takes a lot of patience.

If only I knew not of anger and had no time for it; then I would
not be wound up with all the shit. Gee, I shall learn, I shall learn
quickly, I, I shall not be thick.

A man can walk up a mountain with great ease, but not a child. The love I have only goes so far then that's it, but no matter, I enjoyed the warm and coolness of the day today and the general attacking vibes.

I'm very tired here. I want to sleep. I'm so tired, I need can't sleep. So here I go, goodnight all.
I shall now put down this book.
So off to sleep I fall.

I would really like a girl right now but this will not bring me down and I am not looking for a girl. If one comes then who knows until then nothing.

A friend, a friend to have understanding of me is better than my good lover who will drink me round the bend.

Today I have learned a lesson. Every day for me will be a lesson for every day is a lesson. I must learn it and keep it with me so I know what it's all about.

I want and don't want, I shall be free of want. I shall be able to be free of things and know the joy it brings.

From now, no day will be a waste for every day will there be my lesson of life of which I will truly learn. I will see only what I see and hear only what I hear.

Today, today, today I rest. Sometimes you know this is best. I'm free of the work just sit back, and over your head will go all the crap.

A heavy day today but lessons have been learned. Turks have been Turks so I am still alive, so what more do I want.

Yes, I will. Yes I will live until I die. Whilst I am here I will get on with it the best way I know how and not ask why. When I'm dead then I will look in, and see just where and why I had been.

Now I'm looking forward to hard work and one of the reasons I'm here is to be physically strong as work is mandatory so let's go all out for it. Soon independence will come.

I shall learn from what I see.
I shall come to be me.
It's happening very fast.
I am now together with me at last.

I've not said much today. I've not really wanted to. I've been a bit polluted a lot polluted in my mind but tomorrow is another day.

Yes, I will not want, yet I do know I want. Well, I may well, I may not. I have, I have not.

I'm where I am. I'll see what happens.

Yes, yes always something. I don't know what will happen next, do you?

Watcha friend you fucked up, fucking freak. How you doing? Because I'm doing fucking fine, as fine as your beard. Listen, the days of watcha cock are slowly going son!.

What were the four points of the compass before North, East, South and West were invented?

Guess what, I'm back in holy land yeah, back in Turkey.

Well, yes, well yes, well no, well no. What, pardon me?

Well, I have found a partner in fact millions of partners and they seem to like me, like me. That's why I can't sleep at night and I'm covered in spots.

I don't mind, I don't mind, whatever I do I'm not concerned. I'll travel East, I'll travel west, and I've been south. The West is the best.

What 1 month in pummakaala, they say I'm a mad crazy being!!

White sulphur the spice of life.

A good swim is full of good like the good water off youth only from pamukkale.

I will not age like the sun, I will be like a very thick book without a page.

It ís not, but it is whatever.

Yes, how can you climb a mountain when you can see the higher glimpse, don't do it, stay in the mingle.

Guess what, I slept in a Turkish village in a Turkish house. Yeah. Great. Yeah. It was to know something is learning out for your liberty.

Sleep with the fears you face.
Sleep with the legs, oh yes.
Sleep with the rats, oh yes.
Sleep anywhere, I don't care!

I tried fishing, no way Jose, too much headache; too much confusion.

Fishing for trout, fishing for trout, never mind it's very about.

Another whatever!

What nothing, what nothing at all.
Go, I want nothing, I'm no fool.

A letter said 'Hope it goes well,' I know it will, (do I?)

Well, maybe it will, who knows, who cares, who wins, who dares?

Talk too much and you get a headache, is this worth it?

Maybe, you were well really – who knows? Who knows?

A funny sort of time is now. Really it is – is it?

Oh no, oh yes, the west is the best?

I know I must write something. I must!

If it was, it may not be now. If no wasn't then how is it not now?

Today, tomorrow, who gives a damn?

I do, I don't, I will, I won't, I did, ha, ha, yeah, yeah, yeah.

WARNING

WARNING, WARNING

YOU WILL DIE WITHIN

FROM THESE WRITINGS IF READ WITHOUT THOUGHT
AND JUST UNDERSTANDING, WILL REACH WITHIN YOU
LITTLE BY LITTLE. THE READING WILL BE THE FIRST
BRICK IN THE WALL'S WALL. THEN THE FOUNDATIONS
FOR THIS SHALL GROW IF UNDERSTOOD. SOME PARTS
YOU WILL UNDERSTAND AND OTHERS YOU WILL NOT
BUT IF UNDERSTOOD, AND EXIST, THEN ONE
UNDERSTANDING WILL LED TO ANOTHER.

SLOWLY, SLOWLY.

THERE IS NO TIME, THEREFORE NO RUSH.

YOUR WORLD WILL BE TAKEN APART WITHIN YOU.

I dedicate this book

To all those who wish to

Die within the world.

For those who want to pass

Through this world into

The next whilst

Existing in this one.

For all those who want

To lay down their life

For the truth less truth.

For all those who just

Simply want to be a part of

What is which is what it is.

To entertain yourself on a desert island by yourself takes peace within. I want or rather I need this so I don't have to rely on any television, radio, or people. What I am trying to say is that I want to be out of the world and in myself. I need as well as I want to be one. I must do as I feel and not as in another person's path. But I shall not do as I feel which may hurt anybody intentionally. If I hurt someone then it is a problem that they must overcome so they will; not be hurt again. What I'm trying to say is that if we have nothing to do with each other and just stay with ourselves then there will be no offense. Be part of people but don't take them in and just accept everything people do or say to you, then you will not be hurt. So most of all, have no long-term plan because the world is too unreliable.

Human beings fail to recognise other human beings. What I am trying to say is, but even the worst kind of person is still human. And the reason why they are worst kind of humans is because they often have too much frustration and society does not help them, by encouraging them. So when there is a brawl in the streets more often than not there is encouragement for the fight to be won rather than stopped. And the course of the fight is the click of anger between the fight and the pair. There will one day be no more, then humans will realise that life is sacred and some that live in the world are not truly beautiful. Children are corrupted by society so he loses his inherent childlike manner only to build a hardened shell around himself. May we all be saved to become children once more?

It is for every man to help himself for only he can truly do himself any good, but he also needs to be with his own kind who want to help themselves. So if everybody wanted to help themselves then the world would help each other. To be content means man must look no further than now. The past is gone. We must forget and not dwell on it. The future does not exist and we must not mourn for it. No future, no past then we will just accept the present is being what it is and handling it the best way we know how. Then our minds can be free of what's gone and be free of what has not yet happened. The less of weight we have on our shoulders, the lighter life will be and if there is an easy way out then why not have it. But it is not easy to get there, but when you are there then paradise.

So I believe in keeping the conscience clear of wanting and wanting to receive for what I have done. But I repeat, but it is very hard to work on the basis of I shall not give to receive but merely give to others to give to myself. I'm sure that we all get great feelings from giving so long as the intensions of receiving is not there, but when it is then it becomes profit making business sales) which is a pollutant. When I have a large sum of anything, I don't want to lose it. Therefore I withhold giving very much so I don't lose it, but it will go, but not when I have a little sum of anything and I give all I can. I seem to get more pleasure from giving when I have little than if I have more. Now people would say well, the reason is because if you have little, you have little to lose. Now, if this is true then maybe if we can have little we would give more and be happier for it, maybe.

It is very important never to take people for what they have or what they are in the world of fame or status. It is very important for ourselves as well as for other people to take people seriously as they are. Too often in history and in present a rich man will look down on a poor man and not want to know him because he has nothing, therefore his personality does not count. The very same may be applied vice a versa. But society has made sure that the two rarely mix (what a waste of life). Therefore, there is no understanding between men as men. How will this ever change? Well, it will take down to earthness for people to realise that we are all one, the great one cannot be split if it is then it is false.

Let's not forget that the world is a stage and we all play a part in the spirit of things to help make it work. To be the way that it is, may at the moment it be bad or may be good. But then there are false people like ones who act to suit others and those who pretend to be upper class or lower class, or middle class. The primary objective is only to be yourself, be yourself, step into no other's shoes and don't be a slave to anybody's ideals in the world who think that their way is better than your way. In other words, don't be weak, don't follow others no matter what situations you're in. Be yourself, truly then whoever accepts you for you is your friend. Whoever doesn't does not is not aware that you are on your own path. But remember, never judge anyone for what they are, just accept them, then you are yourself.

Take a deep breath and you will be alright. Take a deep breath and every chaos will calm down. We, or rather I, often babble with people inside my head, what a waste of time and thought. It's so hard to think of good things and ways to control our minds. The answer is unless your thoughts are productive, then don't think at all. How nice it would be if a man could use one language to communicate then they would be not misunderstood or confused. Try to say hello to a stranger who is not really a stranger but another one of you and you will find it difficult but once you have done it then you will feel better for it. But you will be depressed by the sly remarks that your own mind will give you when you must say hello again with the sure confidence and break through the barrier of me and you

Don't get hot-headed or lose your temper with others who lose it at you. Use your temper but control it so there is no battle, because battle often loves resentment, tension. The way to handle it towards each other is to be gentle and graceful as possible. Too often we get panicky when we feel threatened and we lose our heads. But then if we don't build walls then no one can tear them down. Rest at night and think of the day, just the day. If it's been a mental struggle find the piece to solve the struggle of the day. Then believe it from the heart and stay with it. The way to do it is by not thinking about it and don't take it in at the time. Be free of worry, be free of greed, be free of resentment, and be free of anger. Etc. don't carry these. That's the most important is don't pick them up in the first place.

When people put you down and slander you, and are nasty towards you and tell you you're stupid, and all that that people can do, then just tell yourself that you are alright and have faith in that. Do not let people bully you when you have done nothing to them and even if you have then you must suffer yourself, and not by other people. Tell yourself when you are depressed that you are alright and believe it. Then yourself that you will prevail over the matter and be alright and believe it. Tell yourself again and again that everything will be alright. Problems are caused by weak and ignorant minds because the problem is all in the mind and can be changed to better light to be purer of the mind. We must try to make better use of our hearts and minds to make our lives more simple, uncomplicated and more calm and relaxed.

If you truly want to do something for yourself that you trust you know to be good for you, without hurting others, you must first be yourself and understand why you're going to do it. Then believe it. Have faith and no doubt. Don't tell other people and think this is good enough, before you tell people be yourself first. People are not that special that you can give your word to them and keep it without first giving it to yourself. I want to stop smoking, so I told myself why, and when I shall stop. But really told myself and have listened to myself how I can tell other people that I have stopped because I have told myself. If I had told how first without why, myself, then I could have more for them and not for me, and that's not strong enough. Be brave, be true.

Try to have no one carry you in life or if you do then use it to learn how to survive independently if you can. Rely on no one to make the first steps for you, do it for yourself and hope will come to you, then people see you are helping yourself. If you rely on people to carry you through then you will not be true to yourself. Burden no one unless of course, it is very mutual and have understanding between you and them. If there is understanding then you will carry each other and learn by it, but one sidedness does not often work. If a man is unable to carry himself, then help him as you can. Be good have understanding and then you will be rewarded. If a man still does not learn to carry his own weight then it is because you can do nothing for him, so he must be passed onto another, and maybe that other person can teach him where you can't.

Jesus said on the cross "Forgive them Father, for they do not know what they do." This is also true in actions of people today. But we must have understanding of this and realise that people are sometimes preoccupied with something else in their mind and their actions don't do good for anyone, but understand that if men can sit down and realise what is good and I mean genuinely good without self-interest but it's very difficult for men to see this. See always the good in everybody and they are good to you in some way then what ever they do outside of this will have no consequence whatsoever. Understanding of man is vital in the survival of man.

Don't worry. Don't upset other people with your problems or what to do. You will find a door that will open for you when the time is right, then you can step through it and hopefully you will have learned a lesson during your last trial. Learn in your situations before leaving then ensure you have mastered what you learned and a door will open. People who do good things for others are often blind to the fact that they hurt others. People are blind to the fact that they are blind of what they do. You must realize that a lot of people do things that they think are good and that it's been beneficial to others but are in fact doing no good at all. We must realise what is good and know that if we are doing no good to others to stop. But a lot of the time people don't know what they are doing

Try not to have your mind preoccupied with pains or resentments. If you do then the day will be a waste and you will learn <u>nothing</u>. There is really no need to plan because what often happens is that when you plan what you're going to say to somebody and in what expression, it comes out completely different and you say something else. The same goes for when you plan to do something. Life is too short, be mindful to waste it by plans. Let the moment take control then you can control it. Plan for it and anything else that happens you will find it hard or impossible to control. Today I killed lots of wasps, a lot of them without hatred, ego, without power behind killing them what I'm trying to say is that sometimes we must take action without any bad thinking behind it. Never consciously take a life, there is never a need

In the event that man will no longer seek to be wise of worldly ways and ambition to make money, then the world could and will be saved from mass destruction and pain. The need for simple food and water, and love, and just between ourselves to survive. Too many people are weak of mind and cannot control themselves from being led away by society. Such as gambling. If a heavy gambler, unless he is not emotionally involved with it and doesn't put himself mentally into it, will always be a loser and try to gain what he has lost. So for this man, it becomes a business of which he is to be sucked into and do any losing to make his business successful. He will bring himself a lot of pain and to others, and never be content. Do not try to gain what you have not got and you will not lose.

If you have a nice house with lots of things, and you know a robber and he wants to be your friend, bring him over to your house and give him your house. If he steals from you, then you will not bring him there again, yet don't become his enemy. See him in spite of your house, see him in his house but if you like him for a certain quality that he has towards you then he has a friend still. You can be friends with people without making them 100% of your life. See him, know him, be good to him and understand him however remember he is fallible like you and capable of fallible things

Page 45=Blind men are as equally blind, if they cannot see all sides to man. Be a friend to all men and you will not have made judgments on other people and dismissed them for what they do. If you are a killer, some will accept you and some won't. Well thank god that some people do except you or you would die of loneliness.

If somebody needs help with something that they are having difficulty with, but do not ask for it, if you know of an easier way then show them that you know an easier way and leave the rest to them. Don't tell them what to do; show and he will see if he doesn't then He will find his own way sooner or later.

Do not expect anything then there will be no disappointment and want for nothing then you will never be short. A problem is only in the mind because if you do everything with contentment and joy then you will be happy in what you are doing, so the problem will not exist. Too many people look at things or situations as a problem because it becomes boring or they have nothing in return that shows but if you seek pleasure in looking after a severely disabled person that requires a lot of attention then there is no problem. Free your mind of burdens or at least what you think are burdens then be content with situations. And know that you are doing good and believe it with faith. Too many people are not able to see the good side to everybody and only see the negative side but that does not help in being relaxed with yourself. Calm down and look with good possibility and your situation can be resolved without running away.

Feel inside of you what is good and know it. Don't think what is good for the mind this is a distracter of goodness, you must reach deep within your heart and know. Let no man get to you, no matter what he says or does to you. Be free of him where you can. Use what he says or does to you and you know what is good for you and that you are not led astray. Be the true advisor to yourself and let no one be your true master for he has his own path to follow and you have yours. If somebody says to you, "Don't eat like a pig" in company, I can only say, but you are not eating like a pig, you are just eating." You are not a pig. So carry no weight on what people say about you for they are not judges and they probably don't judge themselves.

I will follow the path to be the master of myself. I shall know how to deal with myself when awkwardness arises. But this is a lengthy struggle, but every step is one step closer to an understanding of myself. Once I get half way to understanding me then I am half way there in understanding others. No judgement shall be made of others, merely understanding and non-judgment at them. Why should we walk about in a cloud of unknowing about ourselves, for if we don't, ourselves then we are blind to our very existence. Life is too short for trouble making and it is counterproductive, but learning about ourselves and others can pave way for an easier life for the next lot of people to come which will be beneficial to all who are willing to learn and understand and believe in themselves. Let's be honest with ourselves about which is very true of the best way to live.

Have confidence with yourself. Trust yourself to believe what you see or hear. Never bark with the wolfs unless you know it's what you want to do. But don't be scared not to follow suit with others. Know your mind and believe that anything is possible so you may be prepared for the impossible. Too often people are scared of what they cannot understand, so understand it before it happens. To be ready for it, you must keep an open mind and stout heart. Also, you must have faith in that whatever happens is meant to be because it is happening and has been done. The man who will wait for trouble to end and despairs, truly knows the value of life for he can see a light of good things to come which will enable him to be calm. The knowing of good things shall be able to keep you going and able to see ahead of hard situations. The realisation that nothing stays the same must be waited on with calm patience. But if you can get away from it by running away it will not help.

Man has too often been too cruel to his own kind. But in the old days they used to show off disabled people or freaks in a show, instead of giving love and tolerance to them they obscured them. When a child is born deformed, it is best for you to see how you react, don't pollute your mind by following others and making fun of him, understand him and love him for what he is. Do not forget every bad thing you do to others will always come back on you in one way or another. Never be possessive, never make people or things a passion make them a pleasure but if they go, or someone else takes over, then no jealousy should appear. Hold onto nothing, grip nothing to tightly or you will lose it. Make nothing an obsession then you won't mind when it's gone. Never worry and be jealous of another man's fortune, for what you don't have, just don't want. If it comes, it comes. If it goes, it goes.

If there is a strong wind, go with it for like strong waves on a stormy day, the waves always end up ashore and set free. Don't fight the wind; go with it for like the waves you will end up free. If you fight the storm you will tire and be in frustration. Go with it and you will be moved along. Be free of thinking of fighting and battling, and anger, and fear and fright, and dismiss them. Never hold grudges or plan for another man's disaster. Don't waste the useful space in your head for counter productiveness. Be wise, be brave, be good, learn and make use of what you have learned when the time is right. Don't carry waits, don't pick them up. Stay with yourself, stay with now. Don't seek for business, don' seek for gain and content will begin its course.

If you want a flower to grow and suit you, you must water and look after it for it to be sweet. If you mistreat it, it will grow limp and lose interest because of you. Be careful. Even the meanest man in the world will part with his last penny if he is treated right, this all comes down to how you treat people. Although if you are treated badly, you must still treat another person good and see only goodness in him. Ignore the bad. In the end how you treat people if you know how to, is how you will get on with him.

Too hot, too cold, too misty, too clear, too much, too little, too far, too near, too this, too that, too good, too bad, too clever, too stupid, too happy, too sad. What's all this? What's is this and what's that mean, too much or too little? Throw the ball knock down the skittle. What was it then before it was now? How will it end and begin? What is it for? Chuck it up, it might fall down; it may stay up and go round and round; it does not matter. Who really cares? Who will, who won't, and who really dares? It's all really nothing, it started from nothing, it's all made up, it's all very false, there is no truth, and there are no lies. There is not anything in the skies. Our minds have been twisted, we're all messed up, we must all come down to be bottom of the cup. Empty your mind of all the stresses, lay it down like loads of dresses. It's all in the mind which can be cleared therefore it does not exist, take a deep breath, it will all go away. I'm not taking the piss.

Understand that this book is just what it is in the end if understood. Free of thought will just be what it is and flow as freely as nothing so peace shall prevail.

DON'T THINK LET IT ALL GO.

LET THE WORLD OUT OF YOUR MIND AND JUST BE A PART OF WHAT IT ALL IS.

As I started, I came to realise they were simply tears of joy. I was crying for joy I HAD cracked.

Oh what aoh what a relief. When you find nothing in the world is worth the thought of belief. I know what, oh what a release when you know longer follow their worldly lease.

Oh what a, oh what a pleasant but a pleasant surprise when you can be here, wherever here is and your whole body has no anger. I know what a, oh what a freedom of wait that no longer lies in my mind. No longer to relate find or undefined. Ah that was human that that lied in the, oh what a, I know what a release to just be.

When the thoughts come into your mind if you do not relate to them, then they will go because they are not held onto.

It is the flow of the great roundness, the great turn which moves everything. Therefore be a part of this it requires no thought just understanding. Then you can be free of the falseness and deceit which if you are involved in will suck you dry of the broth. Stay out.

! I shall pass by!

People would say that if we meet again we would of met.

People would say that if we do not meet again that we would not of met.

I say

People would say that as there are words on this paper that a letter has been written. People would say that had no words had of been wrote then nothing would have been written.

I say

I have finally, at last discovered the real truth. I have at last discovered the meaning of life. There is no truth, because everything we say and everything we have put a name to, is merely an invention, made to fall and deceive mankind. And the meaning of life is very hard to find and answer because there is no meaning to life. I beg you to take a deep breath until your mind is all and completely clear of thought. Then look up in the sky thought night and the stars are no longer stars. They just are what they are and to prove one point of man's deceit, this is a star picture of the star now when you look up is this what you see? There is no distance, no time, no space, no nothing, it's all made up. I have proved this to myself or stop and though I know. Take deep breaths until the mind is completely clear, then nothing has a name, there is no reason. These last few weeks I have been doing everything from the heart.

Let me tell you something, the heart does not know everything. Judgement, any despair, any anger, any anything. It's the mind that is Polluter of the heart. If nobody thought then there would be no murder, rape, judgement, wanting, planning, anything. We would all work from the heart and the heart knows no good because good thoughts can be looked at as bad thoughts and vice versa. You would be content with just being what you are, which you don't know because what every man has called you, such as a human being is a liar, because if you grew a child up by himself and you asked him what he was, he would know nothing because his mind would not have been polluted by man's invention of words and judgement. I have found or rather I know that even sex, lust is all in the mind. I know that a woman will feel that she wants

Produce at some time in her life. When she does then she should find a male and make children, then when the baby is born it should be looked after our without thought. We were all born alone and should remain this way with no emotions for other people, we would just do from the heart. We would all be content with ourselves and the whole world if we were non-thinkers that just doers. When the child is old enough to defend itself it goes with no attachments and the man and woman who helped to bring the life in the Earth would just quite simply have nothing more to do with each other. Remember your children are not yours the sun has no claim on the Earth and we have no claim to it.

Judgement. Well what is good and what is bad? Something will happen and 50% of people will say this is good and 50% of people say this is bad. Why? Because in every good thing people see bad, and in every bad thing

People will see good. So what is good and bad? The answer is there is no good or bad only what you think, but whatever you think is good, the bad side can be shown and vice versa. Example. I asked a friend to eat a piece of peach, he did so, then I asked the friend what he thought of it, he said, "Good".

Then I mashed the peach up with my hand and put it on the table and said to him "Have some peach now". He replied, "No it looks HORRIBLE!" So I asked him as a special favour to eat some for me. After a lot of persuasion he had some. "Well" I asked, "How does it taste?" He said he didn't know because he felt embarrassed, but after he said, "It tastes the same". So the lesson is, yes first taste the raw and Apple before you judge it, that even then if it does not taste to your liking, just say it's not to your liking, don't say, "It's bad" because if someone else eight see it and they say it's good then what is it?

By saying something is bad or good you are making a judgement on something you don't fully know the truth about. Okay, it may not be to your liking but taste it first and if you decide you still don't like it then, it's not for you, but don't lie to yourself and keep free for other people to try because it may suit them. "That is your country, this is my country". What a load of nonsense. We are all part of the huge surroundings that surround us. But because man has invented a world and made his own rules, then he will suffer by it. If a man governed himself and only himself without wanting to do or not to do for others, then people would just do instinctively from the heart. The mind is the curse of the world and this is why it is the way it is. The first mistake man made is when he felt he needed to relate to things, and then began to think of names and reasons

For his own existence and everything else. The mind when it gets bored, in other words when man is not content with himself, tends to invent things or find things to do. Now then, our minds are only there to allow us to see what we see here what we hear and taste what we taste, and feel what we feel. And our own instinctive feelings from the heart world tell us not to go that way because their eyes are saying "no", the ears will turn away from a noise it does not approve of. Our taste will tell us, "no thank you" and our feel will say no to touch this or that. Our bellies will tell us when we are hungry (need food) and when we are in need of liquid. But if your eyes tell you it's dangerous, that's not true, it's just not the way. If your ears tell you that's a horrible sound, that's not true, it's just disturbed them. If your taste buds do not expect a certain food or taste it's not disgusting, it just

Does not appeal to your taste buds will stop if you feel something that your body rejects, it's not because it's vulgar that your feelings say "No" and does not approve. When you're barely needs food, you are not hungry, but merely need substance to stay alive. The same with Water. Anything you think is merely a judgement is untrue. Some people will see a tramp and say "Ewe, look at him his vulgar". That if you dress him up, then he will be accepted this is judgement and it is the cause of the world's own deceit. So "forgive them for they know not what they do". It's true. People don't know what's going on, where they truly come from, and what they are a part of. People are not content within to find contentment for them. They need to buy a television, so they buy one and they say that they are now content. The thing breaks down then the contentness goes. So they have to do take it back and they will keep

Buying it back, if you find it within your heart all this crap and worldly nonsense will go. Then man can get round to understanding himself and others. Poor, poor people are caught up in the vicious display, unreal, made up word and he may destroy himself or he may not. I hope man will realise one day that he is only a part of the universe and it should behave like it. Well then he would throw all he has away and want for nothing more than his food and water. The Bible is good as it sounds or is meant to be? It's too much like a storybook and jumps too high to quickly, it should explain more about love thy neighbour and turn the other cheek. But even the Bible is all made up from words which are an invention of the thinking man. And these words from the Bible have caused wars, destroyed love. Understanding it's done all this but not its main objective, is that all man should come together as one.

The reason for this is because they are words, people quite simply misunderstand it. So if people misunderstand the Bible and can't believe it, then is the Bible truly good? A Christian, what is a Christian? It is supposed to be someone who has laid down his life for God, gave up everything to do with himself. So if you have to travel 5 miles to work every morning, and you have £1 to get there, if someone asks you for it, will you give it and walk knowing that God will provide? But who truly does this? Until you can truly live your life like that, and if you must put a name to it, relate to, then call yourself a Christian. That if you don't and you call yourself a Christian, then you are lying to yourself and others who may believe you are but as soon as they see you doing something like not giving the £1, then they will no longer believe you. Say you are if you must name it, say you are a practising Christian, but not a full one. You see the problem with man is that he feels he must be something all believe in something. Why, because he can't handle himself as he really truly is. We stop trying to look for identification is, this is mostly the trouble of our little world. When we can all understand that, yes the world is a stage and like a stage it is all made up. If man still world could be taken apart with him, as I know it can, then he would feel so relieved that he doesn't have to keep up this pretentious nonsense.

Your mind like a toilet fall of faeces, flush well clean get rid of the bits and pieces. Let it go and BMT in mind, then we will be in paradise for all of mankind.

A letter to yourself. Hey have you been passing that parcel lately? I hope so, for sure and four others after all. If you don't pass it then nobody else can, so do it and do it well. Thank you Lord flush the loo.

Pick the grapes on the tree and watch then split in half. It's quite amusing when you think what grapes really are. Do you know what they are? I mean really know, for your sake not for yourself.

Now what they are? I mean really know, for your sake not for yourself.

Say wash ya bin and how much rubbish have you been collecting lately I hope it's...

Do to the touch state of ill health we are unable to send you satisfactorily.

My peace of mind will help me to cope and handle anything that may happen to me. It will lead me down safely through pieces of glass which I cannot see. I would be able to walk on a narrow edge 5000 feet high, no matter to me if I fall from the sky. Come my way and go from me, it's all the same in my peace of mind that's the key. Death has gone from me, I know the true way, my peace of mind doesn't bring think of it or register anything in the sky. I am just being and I am around me is just doing, I am a part of the universe that is just doing. To be truly out of the world you must have nothing to do with people or any of the worldly concerns. The best way to do this is to be living entirely by oneself but this can be hard, so if you first lock yourself away from society, learn your knowledge then return and keep doing this, then you can be alone even in society, but it takes time and effort. To construct a building, first you must start with the first stone. This applies to building up your contentment. Keep to the understanding, then it will build inside you and your foundation will alter after lengthy struggle begins to set that this is a foundation without a foundation, so it cannot be destroyed. It is a wall less wall. Well once you know the truth of the non-truth and that you are a part of the universe, then death means nothing at all. The universe to be part of takes a lot of doing, it implies thoughtless absolutely. No thought, just understanding and the knowing that you are just a part of it. Everything else is made up. What is God?! Well it is the voice inside your of head that leads you to safety and tells you that you will be alright through the world. Even if you do something wrong like steel or something like that, you are forgiven. But you must not

Abuse this and you must listen to the soft forgiving voice that wants no trouble or grief at all. Even if you lose a right arm, or are about to die, you will be led safely through. This is god. To find it you must reach deep within yourself to find it. If you do not live in the world then there is no need for god, but whilst you are in the world you need it. The god of yourself is always there when you need it, it's always on your side that follow it with grace and grace will come will stop don't do bad because you know you will be forgiven, this is wrong to yourself and to others. Although it will always be put right by god. God does not judge and tells you that you will be ok and not to worry and you shall prevail and the truth is the word and you will be ok you can find it. When we make judgements we don't truly know what we are saying or doing that god does that's why he can tell you, "You will be alright".

So there was a man who had many different people inside his head and they all needed feeding, until one day he thought no more.

We should of being just like the universe. Doing to be, no thought behind it, no nothing. Just to hear, feel, taste, smell and see. But it all went wrong, you know it did because the true way is to be a kid. No nothing about anything, just let it all go by, but know we have a hard way there, it's hard to get by. Experience the world but then become a child once more. Put a lead on the world close the door. Never hate, never love, don't waste your time, the stars don't above. Let it just be and you be part of it, don't get roped into the world stay out of the pit.

These are up there in what we call space.

They are just what they are which is nothing at all.

There is no distance between any of the so called stars until you invent it (measurement). If you hold the book away from your eyes so called stars is exactly the same length away and until you realise that there is no measurement, no distance, no farness, no nearness you will be always deceived because man thinks he has to relate to everything, he invents names. We are just part of what we call the Universe, the Milky Way, whatever, which in fact is nameless and really just what we are. Did the sun tell us it is the sun? Did Pluto tell you it is called Pluto? Well, whatever whatever

The man who thinks he's a man and who walks the worldly way, unless he sees the truth and knows the truth has been led astray. From one deceit comes another, from which there is only a hard way out, crumble your world, take it out from your mind. Lay all down and be without. A man on a sinking ship is going to go down, go down, go down, hit the bottom which has no bottom and know that you just are. Don't seek for the moon, just drink your water and don't travel far.

Be rid of worldly ways

Be rid of worldly

Be rid of

Be rid

Be

Even when we travel to the moon there is still no distance or tie. It's all made up to make the world we are in today, which without it. There would be no world as we know it.

If now they say I'm alive and when I'm gone, I'm dead. Do they really know I'm alive? It's all in the head. What time is now and what is it later? What is the time alligator? It's hard they say to walk a thousand miles but what is this? If they didn't tell you, you wouldn't walk it with smiles.

Stay with the

Be the

Know that all is

And you will be

A part of the

And think

As the Gipsy walked only down the Asphalt road with her shrubbery all the borrow she stop and walk along the grass the dust behind her spat up almost above waiting to be released.

Did the sun tell you it's the sun? Did Pluto tell you it is Pluto? Well what's the answer? Who told you, you are a human being? That's right, now who told them and them before them and them before them, before them, before them? Exactly. It's made up. Therefore you are not a human being.

TRY TO SOLVE IT

WALK AWAY FROM IT

IGNORE IT

It's like a leaf on a tree.

It's coming to the ground.

It's not dead but merely starting a new beginning.

Never ending is the circle of life.

Yet always ending to begin.

Everything big comes from that, that is small and everything small grows from that which is big. So where did it begin my friend and where shall it end? Every thought is merely a thought out as you can be thoughtless, then the thoughts do not exist. Everything that was first nothing is now something only in the mind and can be managed, therefore it does not exist. Like the Universe is called the Universe, it's all just a name.

FEAR

Once you have come to realise that every fear, like heights, dark things that appear to look like ghosts or monsters are all in the mind. Once you have the understanding that you are a part of what (the Universe) is and that everything is just what it is, which is nothing until you're mind reinvents it to something, then fear of anything in shape or form or people will no longer exist within you. If you are frightened of the dark, walk through a park dark on your own in the dark and don't think of anything whatsoever. And stay there remembering that you're are a part of nothing and that everything else is nothing, then you will find you have walked through the park unscarred of anything. Faith of course that's a very important part in it. It is essential that you take deep breaths in this case, it will help clear your mind and you are also being part of what you are.

FEAR 2

Once you have come to understand that you are a part of the huge surroundings that surround us (Universe). Then you will realise that your life is unimportant. Every star and sun must one day burn out. There is no stopping it, so give up your life and realise that if you pass through (die). You are just doing what the universe does, what you are a part of. Therefore fear nobody or anything that may be threatening your life, but if you are being a part of the universe within yourself then you would never relate to this. So what would happen to you, would just quite simply happen and you would be nothing. Don't let your mind recognised death, then you will never fear, because you understand what you are which is......

to be in paradise (content, peace within) you have got to give up your life (world) to be part of the nothingness that surrounds us. This is done by non-thought give up your thoughts and no longer think. Empty your mind of the unreal realism you carry inside of you and you will be relieved of yourself and the world's weight of thoughts. I thought will go if you do not relate to it, then it will no longer exist, relate to it and you will be pulled back into deceit. Keep it out, but if it tries to come in don't relate to it and then it has no grounds on which to settle, so it will last and will go away. Then the peace will come with a new. Remember the universe works very well with our full it just does what it does with the flow of the universe. You can be the same if you give up your life and thoughts within you. And understand what you are without knowing.

Stay with the universe. Just think nothing and it will pass you by and what will be will be. Like the universe it just does without doing and what will be only be what it is which is nothing. The free of thoughts and grace will come to you with just the knowing of what shall be done will be done without the thought of knowing. Lay down your life for yourself give up your desires and wants, for this world pathway for you a contentful existence without being anything don't get angry, for it's all in the mind be free of thought and you will be kind to yourself and all around you.

What will be will be.

Be free of thoughts.

Think nothing.

Just be.

See but do not look, turn you will not see.

Hear that do not listen then you will not hear.

Do without doing then you have done nothing.

Be without being then you will be nothing.

Feel without feeling then nothing can harm you.

Love without loving then you will know no despair.

Have without having then there will be no loss or gain.

Give without giving, no return no pain.

Be aware that without being aware then you will be aware of nothing.

Become nothing in order to know nothing, then nothing shall be nothing and you will be nothing and a part of nothing, which can bring us everything. or something but when you become nothing then there is nothing.

From something which is nothing become nothing in order to know something is nothing then become the nothing which you thought was something and it shall be nothing for you to become nothing. Which is only something if you believe it is something which is passed as nothing because the nothing as nothing and only becomes something when you believe it as something before you knew it is nothing, so in order to know nothing you must see something and yourself as nothing to that you and something is nothing. Then nothing will not be something which is nothing. Let all no thoughts which is nothing become nothing then there is nothing.

Just be and know you are a part of what is. Just truly know that and understand that you know this, then you can just be a part of what is within, what you are. But know it and understand it and be by it.

Follow it.

The content by it.

Then you will just be.

What did you say? A land of peace of mind from who did you hear that? Where could this place be? Tell me that this is a fact.

Yes it is a fact, as I stand here it is so. So go and find your peace of mind on the road to the land of peace of mind.

How long can I stand it without city glued folk? Can peace of mind give me a laugh and a joke?

Forget all desires and peace shall prevail.

It is not possible to love mankind just like that. First you must know the first fundamental steps on what love really is. The first step is to first love and accept yourself for what you really are. If you truly do this and understand this, then you may proceed to understand at this (all others). Understand firstly about yourself that whatever you do and whatever you have done is meant to be because it has happened and shall happen. Secondly, do nothing intentionally to hurt anyone, no vindictiveness, no build-up of anger, no resentment etc. But understand that people who do these things are not bad, not even murderers because they have a problem within and if they could see that what they are doing is a waste, but truly see, then they would not do it. Thirdly don't judge anything or anyone is good or bad, nice or not nice, because you will be judging yourself and others. Just except anything people do or say to you, don't judge them, just understand them. These are just a few examples of love, which is also understanding. If you do something that is wrong to other people, but you think it is good and you are blind to this and you are prepared to forgive yourself, then think this of other people. They don't know what they are doing.

Because the stars were not the stars before we made up the name means that everything is really nothing, it's just names and we are to blame.

There is no distance and no time it is all made up and we have become blind.

The sun never gets tired it just nearly burns out. It's all in the mind we could walk a great distance free of thoughts and without perception. Forget time and distance and nothing is impossible for you could walk 1000 miles and each step would be the first this I know is possible. No time means no rush, no distance means no push, no number means no burden, no thought means only contentment and paradise within.

To entertain yourself on a desert island by yourself takes peace within. I want or rather I need this so I don't have to rely on television, radio or people. What I am trying to say is that I want to be part of the world and in myself. I need as well as want to be one. I must do as I feel and not as another person's part, but I shall not do as I feel would hurt somebody intentionally. If I hurt somebody then it is a problem that they must overcome, so they will not be hurt again. What I'm trying to say is that if we have nothing to do with each other and just stay with ourselves then there will be no offence. The part of people, but don't take them in and just accept everything people do or say to you then you will not be hurt and most of all have no long-term plans because the world is too unreliable.

I UNDERSTAND
  I UNDERSTAND
    IF I DON'T UNDERSTAND
      THEN I UNDERSTAND
        I DON'T UNDERSTAND
          I UNDERSTAND I KNOW.

I UNDERSTAND
  I UNDERSTAND
    THAT IF I UNDERSTAND
      I UNDERSTAND
        BECAUSE I KNOW
          I UNDERSTAND
            I UNDERSTAND I KNOW.

I UNDERSTAND   I UNDERSTAND
                     I UNDERSTAND

        I UNDERSTAND
        I UNDERSTAND

        I UNDERSTAND

I UNDERSTAND

KNOW

Where you do not understand if you understand you do not understand then that there is understanding. You do not have to understand to understand if you have understanding but you must understand.

All subconscious thoughts need an answer of understanding.

No I don't understand

But I understand

I don't understand

Yes I understand

Because I know

I understand

I understand I know

Then they will begin at once to disappear and you will be set free.

I know I do not know.

Therefore I understand.

I don't understand.

I know I understand.

I do not know therefore I understand, I do not know therefore I understand.

We all are a part of which is, which Shell be what is, what is, what it is which is.

When you dream get in there and understand what the dream is about while you are dreaming it then you will see.

BECAUSE I KNOW THAT ANYTHING IN THE WORLD IS POSSIBLE AND KNOW THAT I KNOW, THEREFORE I KNOW.

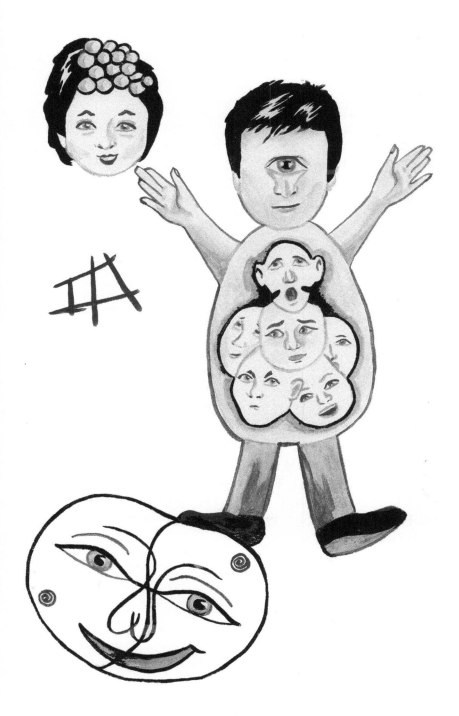

IT IS THE NOTHINGNESS THAT PUTS TOGETHER THE 3 NOTHINGNESSES WHICH MAKES THE EXISTENCE OF NOTHINGNESS

20	21	22	23	24	25	26
20	21	22	23	24	25	26
20	21	22	23	24	25	26
60	63	66	69	72	75	78
6	9	12	15	9	12	15
2x3	3x3		6	3x3	6	6
		4x3	2x3		4x3	3x3

27	28	29	30	31	32	33
27	28	29	30	31	32	33
27	28	29	30	31	32	33
81	84	87	90	93	96	99
9	12	15	9	12	15	18
3x3	4x3	6	3x3	4x3	6	9
		2x3			2x3	3x3

THE EARTH ELEMENT YOU WILL ONLY UNDERSTAND WHEN YOUR MIND IS EMPTY OF THE WORLD AND YOU UNDERSTAND THE NOTHINGNESS. THEN YOU WILL UNDERSTAND AND KNOW THAT EVERY THING THAT IS NOT COMPOSED BY THE 3 ELEMENTS IS MADE BY THE 4TH ELEMENT IS NOT REAL. THE 4TH ELEMENT IS THE NOTHINGNESS AND THE 5TH WHICH PUTS TOGETHER THE 3RD IS THAT.

THERE IS NO HUMAN THINKING WORD FOR THE
FOURTH DIMENSION OTHER THAN IT IS WHAT IT IS
WHICH IS JUST WHAT IT IS.

1	2	3	4	5	6	7	8
1	2	3	4	5	6	7	8
1	2	3	4	5	6	7	8
3	6	9	12	15	18	21	24
	2x3	3x3	4x3	5x3	6x3	3	6
							2x3

THE FORTH
DIMENSION IS THE
NOTHINGNESS
WHICH MAKES THE
ONENESS.

1	2	3	4	5	6	7	8	9	10
1	2	3	4	5	6	7	8	9	10
1	2	3	4	5	6	7	8	9	10
3	6	9	12	15	18	21	24	27	30
	2x3	3x3	4x3	6	9	3	6	9	3
				2x3	3x3		2x3	3x3	

11	12	13	14	15	16	17
11	12	13	14	15	16	17
11	12	13	14	15	16	17
33	36	39	42	45	48	51
6	9	12	6	9	12	6
2x3	3x3	4x3	2x3	3x3	4x3	2x3

18	19
18	19
54	57
9	12
3x4	4x3
18	19

THE FOURTH DIMENSION IS THE
NOTHINGNESS. IF YOU INVENT IT IT
DOES NOT MAKE THE ONENESS.

I want to.

I do not, not want to do.

I do not want to do.

I will do.

It is the nothingness which puts together the 2 nothingness's which makes the existence of the nothingness.

IF A MAN THINKS IT'S BIG   IF A MAN THINKS IT'S SMALL

WHAT'S THE ANSWER?

IF A MAN DOES   IF A MAN DOES

NOT THINK IT'S   NOT THINK IT'S

THEN THE ANSWER IS IT'S?

It is the nothingness which produces the 2 nothingness's, which are put together by the nothingness, which produces the existence of the nothingness, which does what it does by the nothingness which produces the nothingness which causes it to be what it is, which creates the nothingness.

It is the nothingness which produces the 2 nothingness's which are put together by the nothingness, which produces the existence of the nothingness, which does what it does by the nothingness which produces the nothingness, which causes the nothingness to be what the nothingness is; which creates the nothingness – The existence of God.

MIND
KNOWLEDGE
THOUGHT
WORD
UNDERSTAND
KNOW
TRUTH
GOD
EXISTENCE
NOTHING

You have the mind,
To take the knowledge,
To have the thought of,
The word understanding,
To know,
The truth,
Of God which is,
The existence of what is,
Which is,
Nothing.

YOU HAVE THE MIND
TO TAKE THE KNOWLEDGE
TO HAVE THE THOUGHT OF
THE WORD UNDERSTAND
TO KNOW
THE TRUTH
OF GOD WHICH IS
THE EXISTENCE OF WHAT IS
WHICH IS

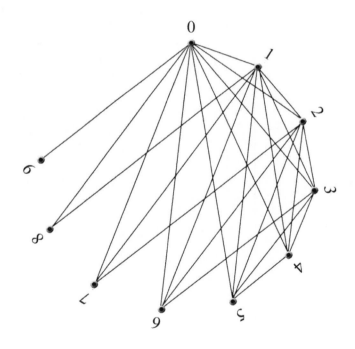

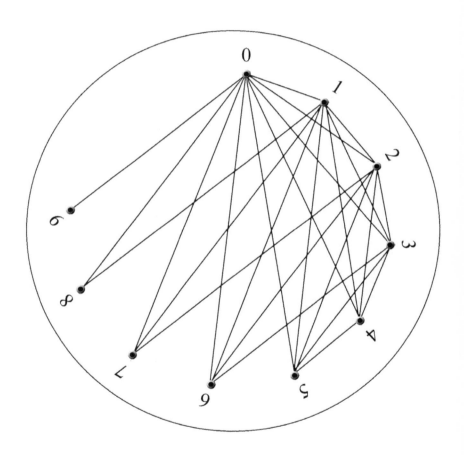

110

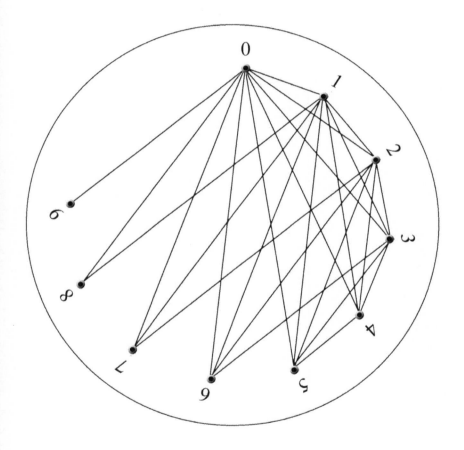

THEY WHICH CAN NOT MAKE A
ONENESS UNTIL THERE IS
UNDERSTANDING.

IT IS ALL A ONENESS
THE RESULT OF WHAT IS
IS THE RESULT OF UNDERSTANDING

SEX = SIN OF THE EXISTENCE.

WE ARE A PART OF THE UNIVERSE.

LIVE OR EXIST LIKE THIS AND YOU WILL BE
CONTENT AND OUT OF THE WORLD OF WHICH
WE HAVE INVENTED.

NOTHING MIND KNOWLEDGE THOUGHT WORD

THE TRUTH OF GOD
DEMANDS RESPECT OF WHICH
I SHALL GIVE.

IF THE SON OF SATAN COMES
HE WILL NOT GIVE FEAR TO PEOPLE
BECUASE THIS MAY ENCOURAGE
THEM TO LOOK FOR GOD, THEREFORE
ALL HE WILL DO IS KEP THEM
AWAY FROM THE TRUTH
OF WHICH HE KNOWS
BUT OPPOSES.

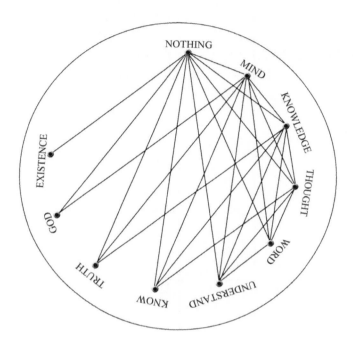

66666 – 666 THE WORLD 6 YOU KNOW 12 ONLY THE
KNOWLEDGE OF 18 GOD OF WHICH YOU GOT FROM
THE PASSING OF 24 THE WORD WHICH IS 30 NOTHING.

MY SACRIFICE IS WHAT MY LORD REQUIRES.
TO MY LORD I SHALL GIVE ALL.
I DO NOT WANT BUT FOR
THE GRACE OF MY MASTER.
BY THE GRACE OF GOD I RECEIVE ONLY THAT
THAT HE HAS TO GIVE.
I SHALL NOT WANT.

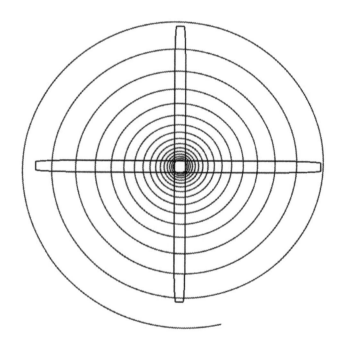

THAT WHICH I DO NOT KNOW AND KNOW I DO NOT
KNOW MEANS THAT ONLY GOD KNOWS THEREFORE I
LEAVE IT TO GOD.

BE CAREFUL. THE WORLD TRIES TO
COME IN BUT KEEP IT OUT.

YOU NEED TO BE STRONG WITH FAITH.

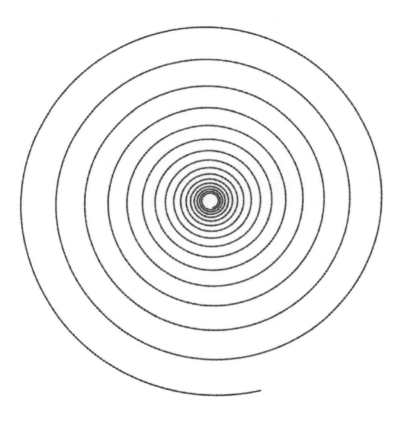

666 is the only distance man has travelled in understanding God. Therefore he creates his own God:

Good and Bad – Pain and Happiness.

Without the true understanding of God, the real Devil – Evil has not yet come.

The man who reaches the full understanding of God and opposes it will keep the 666 going on so people will not know the truth of God, which is 999.

The world which man is trapped in is the 666. When man reaches 999 and follows it, the 666 will be no more. And the man who has 999 and opposes it, is the son of the devil. The man who has the 999 and follows it, is the son of God.

6 you know 12 only the knowledge of 18 God.

9 the existence of 18 God of which 27 is the truth which you know.

6 is the world of which man has created.

9 is the truth of what God is.

If you take the number 9 and add it to itself it was always come back to 9. 6 Will always give you 3, 6, 9 because 6 knows the salt of the existence of God, but 9 is the truth. Therefore it demands it back each time, because it understands the oneness in an older it can reach to the next step every time by adding its own. That's 6 chooses and knows no order of understanding, that always seeks it and goes around the same ground every time.

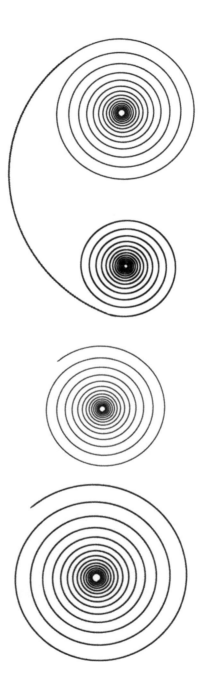

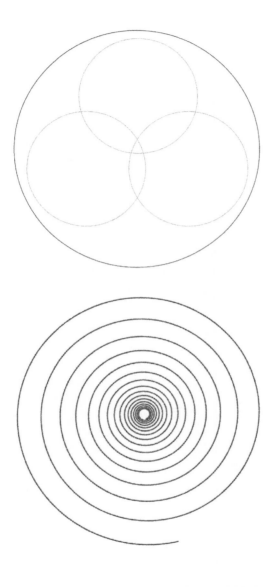

I DO NOT KNOW THE FUTURE AND I KNOW I DO NOT
KNOW THEREFORE I SHALL IMAGINE IT NOT
THEREFORE IT DOES NOT EXIST.

AS THE PAST IS NO LONGER REQUIRED, THEREFORE
I HAVE GIVEN IT TO GOD.

To Eddie,

The Final Note

Yes my friend, stay with the faith and help it for it will help you. No worry for once you know there is no death and no end then nothing matters and you may be set free. The universe will looked after you in its own form, which has no form and you will be led through.

Understand

I cannot enlighten the world by wanting to enlighten the world. I cannot, not enlightenment by not wanting to enlighten the world. I can only enlighten that which I can enlighten.

As I have come to realise that I am nothing and that man only thought up the name. I shall live my life knowing that all in the world are and is false. From now on I see things not as their name, but simply as they are. I no longer see the stars as stars, that as they are. All judgement and worldly ways within me, have now gone, because I know, I know, that the chief is there is no truth and the meaning to life is there is no meaning, only what we have made up which is not true!

At the very top, once you have reached the bottom safe and sound,

When you realise the top is the bottom then you'll know up and down is round and round. But there is no up and down, round and round, no triangles, no sound.

It's all in the mind, made up you see.

It will take you a lot of understanding believe me!

Now I know that there won't be a great white light that will come out from the sky and put everybody in Paradise. Everyone has to find it and want it within themselves. Then they alone can begin the path. In fact another way is if everybody wanted it, then we could all help each other, but I don't think so. So don't wait around for God or man or anything to make you content with yourself and everything. Go and seek it and learn the way to Paradise, it won't be easy and there will be times when you give up, but don't because every step you take is one step nearer.

If I'm honest, I cannot tell people of this truth and make them understand it, unless they are truly looking for it. So shall I dispense with any more talking to people of this level? If however, they are on a journey within themselves to understanding, then I may be able to help them, otherwise no. I also for some time may stop writing, who knows?

The feeling of the understanding I had in Greece is different and was far more powerful because there was really only me. Here is turkey I am once again dumped into society and it is very hard to keep what you have learned alone, preserved in society but after coming back to Greece by myself which I shall be once more. People will always be a distant of clear mindedness because it has a way to make you roped into a thought of absolute uselessness, now the task for me is to be as I was in Greece, in society. Oh what a lengthy struggle of faith. So long as I keep always to the centre of what I know, (in the middle) then I won't go wrong, but too far to the left or right then trouble will begin. That I know I'm wise enough to stay in the middle and not be led astray by society. So my clear mind will prevail.

When people say, "Don't think about it, it will be alright". I don't think they know quite how true and I mean true this is. People say it but do they live by it? People do it but do they know what they're doing? Because if you don't think about it you and it will be all right so don't think anything you think is just a thought and does not truly exist, because you don't think and it goes just like that. Prioritise it and stay with it. If you don't think you will just do what has got to be done, you won't think to get angry, hateful, argumentative, happy, glad, or anything. Therefore you will just be content. Nothing will be able to harm you in any shape or form. Sure you may get robbed, or hit over the head but it still won't harm you. Even if someone close to you dies, but you will have no one close to you in the 1st place. If there, here, there if not here and not that's all. It's called not being human and just a part of the universe.

SO IT
JUST IS WHAT
IT IS WHICH IS JUST WHAT
IT IS WHICH IS JUST
WHAT I SEE
WHICH IS
JUST WHAT IT IS.
THERE FORE IT IS ANYTHING,
NOTHING
OTHER THAN
WHAT IT
IS.

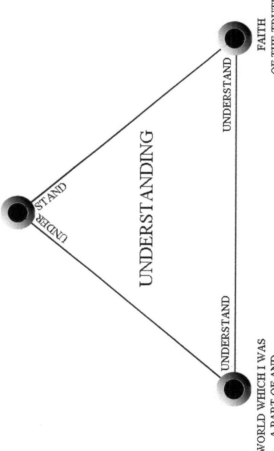

GOD OF WHICH I AM A PART OF

UNDERSTANDING

UNDERSTAND

UNDER STAND

UNDERSTAND

FAITH
OF THE TRUTH
WHIH I SHALL
CARRY AND SHARE.

WORLD WHICH I WAS
A PART OF AND
NOW NO LONGER
AM

I was born as an innocent child. I grew up by society knowing only what it had to show me.

Now I shall grow up once more knowing only what I know and truly understanding that I know why now and I have only to share this with my grace and society, the world will touch no more.

When the whole world truly understands, then the people will all understand the same understanding and the world as we know it will be no more and the truth shall prevail.

I shall no longer think as the world thinks, I shall think of it no more.

The universe does not go on for Infinity! If you start at the point of the moon and travel, you will eventually come back to the point of which you started. Therefore, it goes on forever but always comes back to itself. The unseen force that makes the universe work is the great oneness. The great roundness which churns round and everything in it goes round with it. Therefore, if you start walking around the world in a straight line you will return to the beginning, man will never be able to travel long enough to space in a machine to prove this. I have been there by being a part of the universe and completely out of the world and no longer a human being. The great force that churns the universe around is faster than the speed of light, is the speed of a nature, man cannot understand. Everything is round because the university itself is round. How it goes round, I cannot explain and why it's there has no answer, it just does what it does and that is it.

I shall blame no more.

I shall lay no blame on anybody.

I shall seek not for revenge or carry with a bitter tongue.

I shall thank always my lord for what I have received and for what I have done.

I shall either announce you or deny you as a question or an answer until at which time there is true understanding of which I may plant the seed of the knowledge for the mind. To receive the world to understand, to know the truth of nothing which is the existence of God.

I thank you my sweet lord for the blessing and understanding of the Trinity of which I have solemnly laid my life down for and now shall carry with me your eternal grace.

Now I shall be led through safely with your guiding hand and your spirit within me until I pass through this existence to the next.

I shall pass no judgement, only of what you know.

I shall know of no self-interest. I shall either beg, borrow or steal.

I shall have no female partner of which sex shall be had.

I shall speak only the truth.

I know only the truth, I shall speak not of what I do not know.

There is no true solidness other than the true solidness of understanding. Which is the understanding of God.

Only God knows the true meaning of life, so leave it to him and do not create the idea.

Only God knows the truth of how the universe works and was created, so leave it to him and do not create an idea.

Only God has the understanding of the oneness and has it to share with you, so do not try to find it, it will be given if you take the seed in the mind to have the thought of the word "understand" to know the truth of nothing, which is the existence of God.

Once you truly know and understand that only God knows, then you too will know.

I want to know more other than to be in the hands of God.

I understand truly that that surrounds me, I exist as part of that which exist which is the surroundings that I know have not been thought of, but is the result of understanding. Therefore, I understand I exist as a part of understanding through my understanding. I am aware of my existence by the reflection of water and all other existence of understanding. I exist without the mind to recognise that I am my understanding allows need to be aware of my existence through the awareness of my true surroundings. I understand the existence of other existences, therefore I exist as a part of existence. Before I had the mind to think, my thinking is tied distract her of the truth, my thinking is my enemy of God and has understandings that he has to share with me. Therefore, I exist as an existence of and as part of all existences without the think. I exist truly as nothing through the emptiness of my mind, through this gives me the understanding of truth, that I existing as one with the oneness of an existence of understanding and not as a part of that, that I think or that, that has been thought of!

I exist truly as nothing through the emptiness of my mind, through this gives me the understanding of truth, that I existing as one with the oneness of an existence of understanding and not as a part of that, that I think or that, that has been thought of!

I am free from doubt, my understanding as truth giving up unto me from God. I have no reason to doubt what I do not know.

I understand that I do not know, so I leave the knowing to God until he allows me to know. Therefore, I have no doubt in my mind or heart I do not know, therefore God knows.

I know, therefore God has given unto me a blessing of understanding, I do not create an idea that I know for that is straying from God. I wait until he allows me to know all I should. Meanwhile, I lay in the bliss of knowing nothing and I have the knowing that I do not know and I shall obey.

THOUGHTS OF UNDERSTANDING FROM NEGATIVE ELECTRICITY = 0 <u>NEGATIVE</u>
ETERNAL

SEEING AND DOING FROM NEGATIVE ELECTRICITY = O <u>NEGATIVE</u>
ETERNAL

NEGATIVE STATEMENTS OF POSITIVITY FROM N. ELECTRICITY = O <u>NEGATIVE</u>
ETERNAL

EXISTING UNDER AND WITH N. ELECTRICITY = ETERNAL = NON THINKING

THINKING OF KNOWING OR UNDERSTANDING FROM POSITIVE ELECTRICITY = <u>1 POSITIVE</u>
MORTAL

SEEING AND DOING FROM POSITIVE ELECTRICITY = <u>1 POSITIVE</u>
MORTAL

POSITIVE STATEMENTS OF NEGATIVITY FROM P. ELECTRICITY = <u>1 POSITIVE</u>
MORTAL

①P.E. <u>⓪NE</u> ①<u>P.E</u> = DEATH <u>⓪NE</u> = IMMORTAL
ETERNAL MORTAL ETERNAL (NON SELF DESTRUCTIVE)

IMMORTALITY IS POSSIBLE ON THE GROUNDS THAT THERE IS NO OUTSIDE ELEMENT THAT KILLS –EXP JESUS WOULD OF STILL BEEN HERE TODAY IN THE FLESH (RATHER THAN IN SPIRIT FORM) HAD HE NOT OF INTERFERED WITH THE OUTSIDE interference.
LIVING UNDER AND WITH P. ELECTRICITY = MORTAL = THINKING

TWO CHOICES TO MAN = ① TO BE A THINKING LIVING BEING = DEATH UNDER POSITIVE

② TO BE A NON THINKING EXISTING BEING = LIFE UNDER NEGATIVE

MAN SHALL NOT HAVE MORTALITY AS A NEGATIVE LIVING HUMAN BEING.

MAN SHALL HAVE IMMORTALITY AS A NEGATIVE POSITIVE LIVING HUMAN BEING.

MAN SHALL NOT HAVE IMMORTALITY AS LONG AS HE DOES WHAT HE DOES NOT NEED TO TRULY DO.

MAN SHALL HAVE IMMORTALITY AS LONG AS HE DOES WHAT HE TRULY NEEDS TO DO. AND THIS SHALL BE KNOWN WITHIN THE NEGATIVE FIELD OF ELECTRICITY.

WITHIN THE POSITIVE FIELD OF ELECTRICITY A MAN DOES NOT KNOW TRULY WHAT HE NEEDS TO DO.

THINKING = HUGE LOSS OF ELECTRICITY AND HUGE USE OF BLOOD WHICH CARRIES THE BLOOD AWAY FROM WHERE BLOOD NEEDS TO BE.

KNOWING = NO ELECTRICITY USED, AND ALL BLOOD MAY STAY WHERE THE BLOOD NEEDS TO STAY.

AFTER ALL KNOWN IN TRUTH AND EACH STEP JUSTIFIED

THE LIVING ON THIS PLANET MUST BE ONLY TO LOVE

ALL AND KNOW THE POTENTIAL ABILITY OF EVERY
MAN

WOMAN TO ENDANGER YOURSELF MEANS TO
ENDANGER

THE LOVE YOU CAN GIVE TO OTHERS.

HOWEVER DO NOT LOOK TO LOVE PEOPLE

JUST LOVE ALL WHO CROSS YOUR PATH IN

YOU'RE PATH.

TIME TRAVEL

The physical aspect of time travel back to any part is impossible, on the grounds that there will have to be a power that could in some way bring back all the dead, all that, that has been destroyed and there is no such human male (or shall be) power to do that, and there is no power outside of living humans that could do that. A man has the power to bring back a man who is dead, so long as his body is not fully decomposed or rotted, or worse. A man can only work with what he sees and with what is available. A man can turn a glass of water into many pints, yet he cannot turn an empty glass into water. So a man cannot see an all that has been destroyed, so he cannot bring back the past physically or travel back. Plus – there are no days, no numbers, no years, no months, no weeks, and no time, so where could you travel back to? The answer is you can go back in time only in your mind because that's where time (as hours and minutes, etc.) is. The possibility of forward time travel, is only possible if we undergo cryogenics for say 200 years, or travel far away from earth, then return. There is no <u>solid</u> matter that will stay intact, were you to attempt to send the matter into light speed, the matter no matter how strong the object will appear to be, the matter will burn up at a very high speed, therefore solid matter cannot reach light speed.

TO GOD I SHALL GIVE ALL MY
WORLDLY THOUGHTS, AND TO ME HE SHALL
PASS ONLY UNDERSTANDING OF WHICH THEN
I MAY HAVE THOUGHTS OF UNDERSTANDING

I THANK YOU MY SWEET LORD FOR YOUR
UNDERSTANDING

WHEN IT IS TIME IN GOD'S TIME FOR ME TO GO OUT
ONCE AGAIN IN THE WORLD, I WILL TAKE WITH ME
ALL HE HAS GIVEN UNTO ME AND SHARE IN THE WAY
ONLY HE KNOWS HOW. AND PEACE WITHIN ME SHALL
PREVAIL.

I ask you to say not a prayer for me but for your own release into the kingdom of heaven, for, it is for your sins that you die. The pain and suffering of your weakness to your reason and way of thinking may end when you know how all that came to you in misery and despair, false happiness's that lasted maybe well you know that, that happiness was turned away by another intruder. Pray that you may be blessed with the will to understand all three levels. The 4th and 5th will be the result of this work is immortality within the kings domain of heaven where only innocents prevail.

A mistake is based on the perception of perfection in knowing all things are not perfect and there can be a higher entity, therefore there are only errors that are made and no mistakes as we do not know the outcome.

The positive electricity used to make positive statements is in fact negative. So the electricity burns out – the negative electricity used is in fact positive and uses no electricity so the electricity is spared. Hence for every negative statement made for a positive means that the electricity spared may be used for a higher electricity over a long period of time. To look without looking means you save a quantity of electricity. There is no electricity used in naturally seeing however there is plenty used in looking.

CONSCIENCELY LOOKING = <u>POSITIVE ELECTRICITY</u>.
NON-CONSCIENCELY SEEING = <u>NEGATIVE ELECTRICITY!</u>

Because the brain is small yet bigger in depth and in space than the universe means that all is all is within reach in terms of to the greater the power for a man to be outside of all that is all of irrelevant, and to be able to touch all the forces of power from the universe and 0-point energy levels.

The mind of a man is so potentially great that all levels of 0-point may hammer through him, which potentially may allow him to exercise any amount of power through 0-point. Example = turn on any = turn on – off any – move any – heal any = X2 etc., any = create any.

The 100% use of the brain means to be completely with god.

To think you have won means you can think you have lost, lost or loose does not exist as true words. When you put £10 on a horse and the horse does not come first, you have not lost the ten pounds because you know where the ten pounds went and you did not lose, for the £10 of change simply took the money away. And because the ten pounds is still on your mind after the event, means the ten pounds is still there. And when you can no longer remember that occasion means the memory of that was taken away. To understand that you cannot lose means you must sacrifice your meaning of win. Then you can never lose. To have nothing to lose means you have no attachment of things to you. To lose or to have lost nothing is impossible for you may become blind to nothing or you may have your memory taken away by the flow of life. Never consider you have won then you shall not lose.

In fact you cannot lose anything because you can always track the thing!

BE IGNORANT OF THE WORLD AND WISE IN THE KINGDOM OF HEAVEN.

TO BE IGNORANT OF THE KINGDOM OF HEAVEN IS NOT BLISS.

TO THINK WISDOM IS FOLLY – THIS IS FOLLY.

THEREFORE THE SAYING –

IF IGNORANCE IS BLISS THEN TO BE WISE IS FOLLY IS INCORRECT! YOU HAVE TO BE WISE OF THE DANGERS AND PERILS OF LIFE SO THAT YOU MAY STAY IGNORANT OF THEM!

Jesus did not or does not suffer pain. For in his mind would be no place to suffer pain, he takes the pain without taking the pain in his mind, therefore there is no pain. For only the devil gives himself pain for he does not know how to overcome pain. For to overcome pain he must take the pain physically yet not mentally.

This way he may endure great undertakings of torture with a smile on our face because you would not be here with the pain. To do this takes great understanding and to be with God is the way to endure pain. Therefore Jesus knew and knows the way to overcome pain and he knows that this would set an example of how to free yourself from pain and this is Good, so why would he have suffered pain when he knows, and knows he knows that this is counterproductive? So when he does not know any pain, there will be the possibility that other men would want this and say "How does he not suffer any pain, how could we be with him in that?" And this is productive.

147

TRUE LOVE = FORMAT

TO LOVE + SUFFER BECAUSE OF CIRCUMSTANCES BUT NEVER LET THE ONE YOU LOVE KNOW IN ORDER TO KEEP THEIR PEACE OF MIND WITH YOU. THEN THEY MAY NEVER BE DISCOURAGED FROM SEEING YOU. (NO BURDEN). YOU MAY ALWAYS SERVE UNSELFISHLY TOWARDS THEM. YOU MAY ALWAYS BE ON THEIR LEVEL WITH 100% UNDERSTANDING OF THEIR POSITIONS AND IDIOSYNCRASIES. THE SERIOUSNESS OF THEM MUST BE RENDERED TO THE HIGHEST. TO GIVE YOU LIFE TO THEM MUST BE TO DEATH WITH WILLINGNESS OF DEATH. BE FOR THEM BE WITH THEM WHENEVER, CAN STANDBY? WARNING – WHEN WITH ANOTHER PARTNER, PAIN EXCEEDS TO 200% OR + STRENGTH LEVEL ++%100.

NEVER GIVE ANY CONNOTATIONS TOWARDS YOURSELF = TO LIVE WITH KISS. GENTLE ALWAYS – FIRMNESS TO.

ALL THAT IS POSSIBLE TO HAPPEN HAS HAPPENED.

ALL THAT IS POSSIBLE TO COME IS POSSIBLE BUT NOT CERTAIN.

AND MAN THAT DOES NOT BELIEVE ALL TO BE POSSIBLE

AND SAYS YOU SHOULD USE THE TERMINOLOGY "ALL WAS POSSIBLE." CAN NOT SAY THAT ON THE GROUNDS THAT, SHOULD HE TODAY NOT BELIEVE THAT ALL IS POSSIBLE THEN HOW COULD HE OF BELIEVED THAT LANDING ON THE MOON "WAS" POSSIBLE IN THE 15TH CENTURY?

LET ALL MEN WHO
FEAR DEATH, DIE.
SO THAT THEY MAY NOT
FEAR THE LOSS OF WHAT
THE DEVIL WANTS TO
KEEP.

Love beith not selfish, nor self-destructive and most certainly not self-superficial, for love does that and causes no harm for love is peace.

UNDER SECTION OF SPEECH – 217.5. PH.7. THE NEGATIVE ENERGY OF THE WORLD IF IS NOT THAT OF THE POSITIVITY AND STATES NO CERTAINTY.

SECTION 1 – 2 HAVE BEEN PLACED IN ORDER OF LAW 127.4 AND ARE IN OPERATION. ANY USE WILL AND SHALL RESULT IN PENALTY 494 UNDER SECTION 2 OF THE CONSCIENCE ACT.

EVERY EFFORT TO UPHOLD THE NEGATIVE LAW SHALL BE ASSISTED BY TWO STEPS.

I thank myself for what I have given because I'm not going to punish myself.

I do not thank anybody for what they have given me, for I do not know who I'm thanking, and maybe he will punish himself for what he has given me and I do not want to thank him for that.

I do not say thank you to him and he takes what he gave away, then I say thank you, for he may learn what the true meaning of giving is.

WITHIN THE PURITY OF NOTHINGNESS LAYS AN UNDERSTAND WHICH IS CAPABLE OF MAKING ANY SUCH HAPPENING POSSIBLE!

FROM NOTHINGNESS COMES TRUTH

MY FAITH IN GOD ALLOWS
ME FORGIVENESS TO ALL WHO
COMMIT WORLDLY ACTIONS.
MY HOPE IS THAT ALL WILL
KNOW GOD. SO I SHALL NOT
JUDGE THEM.

MY CHARITY IS MY UNDERSTANDING
OF JESUS CHRIST.

MY LORD, I PRAY ALL WILL KNOW YOU
AS I DO. I PRAY ALL WILL FOLLOW
JESUS CHRIST.

I PRAY THE WORLD MAY
BE SAVED, LEFT IN YOUR
UNDERSTANDING.

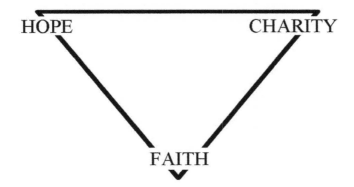

When you have hope then you understand. Your hope is for all to know God, and those who do actions that are not of God, then you have the hope that they will know you and you will not judge them. Because your faith is strong to understand them and your charity is the understanding.

Because you have the faith to know, that, if a man makes actions that are not for God, then you know he has fallen in the eyes of God and because you have hope that all will know God, you will not judge them.

And your charity is your understanding of God.

FAITH = FORGIVENESS for they know not what they do.

HOPE = FOR GOD that all will know God.

CHARITY = UNDERSTANDING of God which is forgiveness and hope that all shall know him.

1. God will give you only what you need, the temptations of the devil will make

2. Know and know that you know, that which is good for your mind, soul, and heart and for the good of God. Keep a clear mind and soul of the world's way of thinking.

3. Understand the spirit of Jesus.

---

1. When you are open to temptation then the devil will be quick to tempt you. Once you have been tempted and gone through the process of throwing out the temptation from your soul then you become higher with god spiritually.

2. The deal that you have done spiritually that demands the physical action to complete Gods understanding about the devil.

3. Do the deed physically then in the devils hands you are allowed to make mistakes but only to learn from them to be free from the devil.

All things that are outside of the mirror are in fact the reflection of the mirror. Hence are not pure. The mirror is pure to the point that the mirror only exists and has no control over what he sees. When man becomes the mirror then he sees all things and man as an opposite reflection.

TEXT UNDER SECTION 479298 Ph.4

<u>MEDIUMS</u> – Voice from the Dead

Once a person goes to the grave, then they become nothing, they become part of nothing with no power to come back and that person who goes to the grave never really existed as a true spirit, he lived as a man-made character, so you cannot communicate with what does not exist and with what is not there. When people are to be their true selves and not made up, then this will be different.

The goal keeper's job is to defend the ball.

The devil's job is to defend his selfish.

Become the goal keeper's friend and you can put the ball in the goal indirectly. Ask the goal keeper to let you put the ball in the goal as a direct shooter, would be too much of a big step for him. Expose the devil's character directly and this becomes too much and he must become his friend and you may expose him in time with grace. When the ball is put past the keeper indirectly enough times, he will learn that his effort to defend shall not be necessary. Expose the devil gradually as his friend indirectly then he shall see himself and shall have the knowledge of the devil at hand, to change himself to a better being. Direct attack can work but at the same time the person but must be very vulnerable ad ready to give in. Other than that he will keep defending his right to be who he has made himself to be even after direct attacking. Only 5% (total % of all people to defend = 95%) would agree and be set for change.

Rule 17.6 Ph.4a sub rule and Section (not listed) for sect-

All events must and shall be that of a productive and more beautiful nature towards me and other people, escalating towards a more graceful nature. The putting in other "people's shoes" is that of a higher entity under section 5470 Ph.5.5 Sub section 654.

The rules may be read under Code 4 of Ph. Sect 564.

LAW

Under Section 5104265 – 5a

I must at a time that's productive and practical give up that that I know to be good, as a living being in order to keep a better peace. So lonely as I know that my action is not really what I want to do, it keeps peace until I find the break to relieve myself from the situation. And so long as what I do is not directly harmful as physical or mental then I may proceed. I must not wilfully want to do the act first hand, yet when the wind blows against my direction then to fight against the wind means you are only to stumble all the time and fall over. So I must follow the wind until the break comes then I may leave. Shall the act be morally, or physically or mentally harmful in the long term, then the other person who commits the acts shall be the punisher, because he is the one who wants, and I either want or do not, not, want. I shall go with the wind until I can be free yet shall be trapped. Even though my conscious of moral standards are afraid to do the act willingly. I must sacrifice my morals for the greater peace. To say no when I'm in debt shall only bring guilt to me. So I must accept that the peace of life that I'm committing to is a productive nature and shall not last. To say no, then cannot to the life, brings dismay. To say yes, but that is not really what I want, but until the debt is paid, then I shall commit the life knowing but that life is not me, yet I'm buying peace. Jump into the wind, and worry not for you shall justify your own will for this is a protection in you piece status.

Unless I can fully escape the situation then I must give in. And you should just say I'm not going to do this anymore, with your will until your mind is settles about what you are going to say.

For all you know of things is your own death to the grave. The things of many are the things of energy which waste away in your mind. So you are brought down to the grave. The weight of or wanting of things is your own oldness you give into yourself, the acknowledgement of 1-2-3 time puts you into a climax of a last breath. The willing of rain to come which is not in your control shall lay you to rest for interfering with purity. The hoping for wellbeing on Friday shall finish your soul to dust. All your thinking of others shall allow your heart to be tired and so stop.

In the Kingdom of Heaven you are one with God therefore –
prayers are not necessary and wishes are very powerful. However,
you must always give praise and thanks for all great deeds done
and given in the world. Prayers are more powerful than wishes
(only 3 are given) however a prayer must be not often and of
humble ask and very necessary.

MANKIND HAS ONLY LEARNED 10% OF THEIR BRAINS
– THEREFORE THEY CAN ONLY USE 10% AND LEARNS
WITHIN THE BOUNDARIES OF 10% LIMITED.

EVERY SINGLE CHILD BORN

EVERY SINGLE HUMAN KILLED

EVERY SINGLE HUMAN THAT HAS DIED – AND HAS THE
POTENTIAL TO HAVE G.P.O.E.

WHAT YOU ARE A PART OF

WORLD
WHICH YOU
ARE A PART OF

THE NOTHINGNESS

GOD   ## THE TRUTH

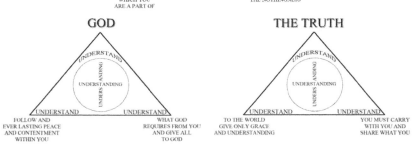

FOLLOW AND
EVER LASTING PEACE
AND CONTENTMENT
WITHIN YOU

WHAT GOD
REQUIRES FROM YOU
AND GIVE ALL
TO GOD

TO THE WORLD
GIVE ONLY GRACE
AND UNDERSTANDING

YOU MUST CARRY
WITH YOU AND
SHARE WHAT YOU

THE UNDERSTANDING OF

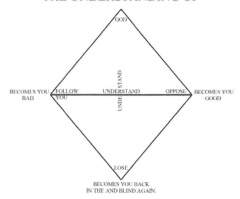

BECOMES YOU
BAD

BECOMES YOU
GOOD

BECOMES YOU BACK
IN THE AND BLIND AGAIN.

164

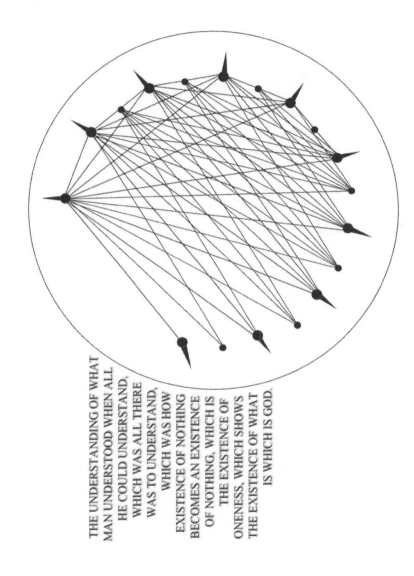

THE UNDERSTANDING OF WHAT
MAN UNDERSTOOD WHEN ALL
HE COULD UNDERSTAND,
WHICH WAS ALL THERE
WAS TO UNDERSTAND,
WHICH WAS HOW
EXISTENCE OF NOTHING
BECOMES AN EXISTENCE
OF NOTHING, WHICH IS
THE EXISTENCE OF
ONENESS, WHICH SHOWS
THE EXISTENCE OF WHAT
IS WHICH IS GOD.

165

WHEN MAN FIRST DID SOMETHING FOR HIMSELF/ HENCE THE WORLD BEGAN HENCE/ 666.

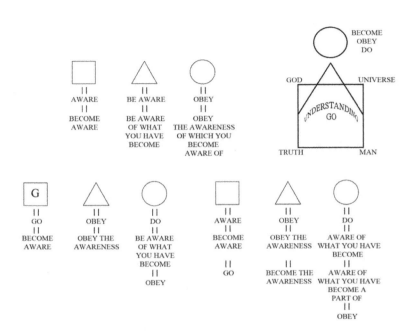

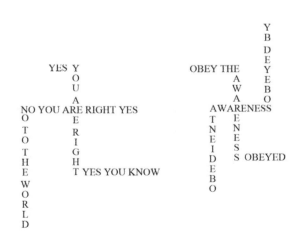

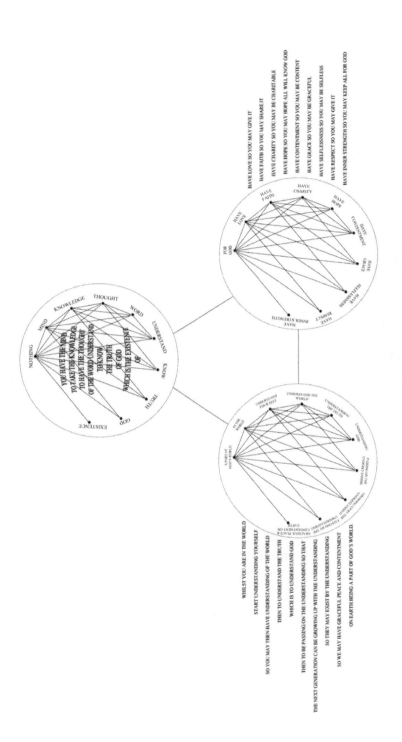

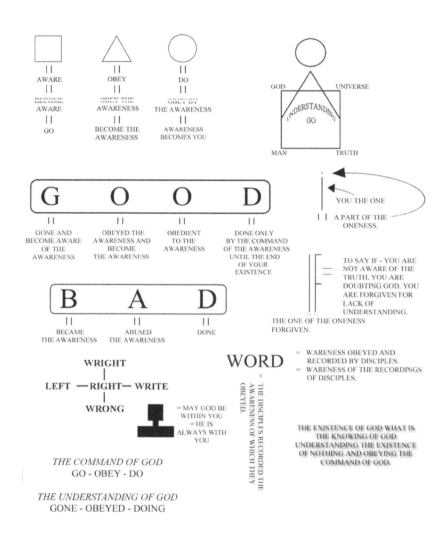

□ = AWARE = BECOME AWARE = GO

△ = OBEY = OBEY THE AWARENESS = BECOME THE AWARENESS

○ = DO = OBEY BY THE AWARENESS = AWARENESS BECOMES YOU

GOD — UNIVERSE
UNDERSTANDING GO
MAN — TRUTH

G O O D

G = GONE AND BECOME AWARE OF THE AWARENESS

O = OBEYED THE AWARENESS AND BECOME THE AWARENESS

O = OBEDIENT TO THE AWARENESS

D = DONE ONLY BY THE COMMAND OF THE AWARENESS UNTIL THE END OF YOUR EXISTENCE

YOU THE ONE
A PART OF THE ONENESS.

B A D

B = BECAME THE AWARENESS

A = ABUSED THE AWARENESS

D = DONE

TO SAY IF - YOU ARE NOT AWARE OF THE TRUTH, YOU ARE DOUBTING GOD, YOU ARE FORGIVEN FOR LACK OF UNDERSTANDING.

THE ONE OF THE ONENESS FORGIVEN.

WRIGHT
LEFT —RIGHT— WRITE
WRONG

WORD
= AWARENESS OBEYED AND RECORDED BY DISCIPLES.
= AWARENESS OF THE RECORDINGS OF DISCIPLES.

= MAY GOD BE WITHIN YOU
= HE IS ALWAYS WITH YOU

THE DISCIPLES RECORDED THE AWARENESS OF WHICH THEY OBEYED.

THE EXISTENCE OF GOD WHAT IS THE KNOWING OF GOD UNDERSTANDING THE EXISTENCE OF NOTHING AND OBEYING THE COMMAND OF GOD.

THE COMMAND OF GOD
GO - OBEY - DO

THE UNDERSTANDING OF GOD
GONE - OBEYED - DOING

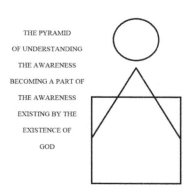

THE PYRAMID
OF UNDERSTANDING
THE AWARENESS
BECOMING A PART OF
THE AWARENESS
EXISTING BY THE
EXISTENCE OF
GOD

THE   REPRESENTS THE 4 UNDERSTANDINGS OF THE UNDERSTANDING OF GOD

THE △ REPRESENTS THE WAY TO GET THE UNDERSTANDING

THE ○ REPRESENTS THE EXISTENCE OF THE UNDERSTANDING

THE □ REPRESNTS AWARENESS OF THE UNDERSATNINDG

THE △ REPRESENTS THE HAVING OF THE UNDERESTANDING

THE ○ REPRESENTS WHERE THE UNDERSTANDING COMES FROM

THE □ REPRESNTS BE AWARE OF THE UNDERSTANDINGS

THE △ REPRESNTS GO BECOME AWARE OF HTE UNDERSTANDING

THE ○ REPRESNTS OBEY THE AWARENESS OBECOME THE UNDERSTANDING

THE △ REPRESNTS DO BY THE UNDERSTANDING

THE □ REPRESNTS YOU HAVE THE 4 ELEMENTS OF UNDERSTANDING

THE ○ REPRESNTS OBEDIENCE TO THE UNDERSETANDING

THE △ REPRESNTS THE TRINITY OF GOD OF WHICH
     □ YOU DO BY I YOUR EXISTECNCE UNTIL YOU PASS THROUGH

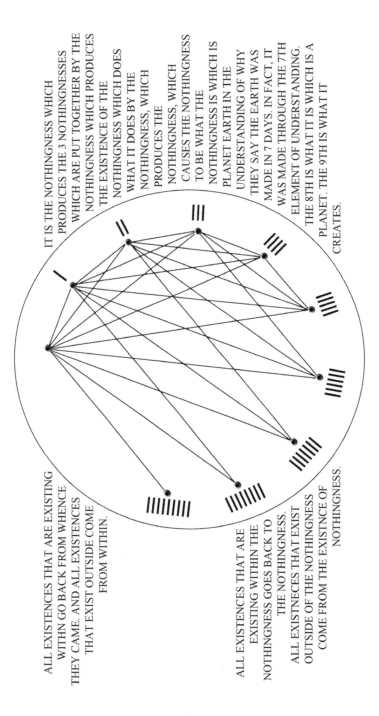

IT IS THE NOTHINGNESS WHICH PRODUCES THE 3 NOTHINGNESSES WHICH ARE PUT TOGETHER BY THE NOTHINGNESS WHICH PRODUCES THE EXISTENCE OF THE NOTHINGNESS WHICH DOES WHAT IT DOES BY THE NOTHINGNESS, WHICH PRODUCES THE NOTHINGNESS, WHICH CAUSES THE NOTHINGNESS TO BE WHAT THE NOTHINGNESS IS WHICH IS PLANET EARTH IN THE UNDERSTANDING OF WHY THEY SAY THE EARTH WAS MADE IN 7 DAYS. IN FACT, IT WAS MADE THROUGH THE 7TH ELEMENT OF UNDERSTANDING. THE 8TH IS WHAT IT IS WHICH IS A PLANET. THE 9TH IS WHAT IT CREATES.

ALL EXISTENCES THAT ARE EXISTING WITHN GO BACK FROM WHENCE THEY CAME. AND ALL EXISTENCES THAT EXIST OUTSIDE COME FROM WITHIN.

ALL EXISTENCES THAT ARE EXISTING WITHIN THE NOTHINGNESS GOES BACK TO THE NOTHINGNESS. ALL EXISTNECES THAT EXIST OUTSIDE OF THE NOTHINGNESS COME FROM THE EXISTNCE OF NOTHINGNESS.

170

IT IS THE NOTHINGNESS WHICH PRODUCES THE 3 NOTHINGNESSES WHICH ARE PUT TOGETHER BY THE NOTHINGNESS, WHICH PRODUCES THE EXISTENCE OF THE NOTHINGNESS, WHICH DOES WHAT IT DOES BY THE NOTHINGNESS, WHICH PRODUCES THE NOTHINGNESS, THE START OF AN EXISTENCE, WHICH CAUSES THE NOTHINGESS TO BE WHAT THE NOTHINGNESS IS, A CREATION OF AN EXISTENCE.

WHICH CREATES
THE NOTHINGNESS
THE LIVING PLANET
EARTH

THE TEN COMMANDMENTS OR NOT THE TEN COMMANDMENTS. IT IS 9 ELEMENTS OF UNDERSTANDING, UNDERSTAND THESE AND YOU WILL BECOME ONE AS A PART OF THE $0 = \frac{GOD}{10}$

ADAM 733?
ADAM AND EVE REPRESENTS THE FIRST BUT AS THE BIBLE CLAIMS ADAM AND EVE TO BE, IS NOT TRUE OR HOW IT IS WRITTEN, BUT IT IS TRUE IN THE FACT THAT IT REPRESENTS THE FIRST PEOPLE WHO WERE HERE. NOW THE FIRST PEOPLE WHO WERE HERE KNEW NOTHING IN ITS REAL SENSE, GOD WAS ABLE TO GET ON WITH HIS WORK, AND ALL THEY WOULD HAVE KNOWN WOULD HAVE BEEN THE EXISTENCE. HENCE THEY WOULD HAVE EXISTED PURELY ON UNDERSTANDING SO THEY WOULD HAVE LIVED FOR AS LONG AS THEY SAY ADAM DID, BUT AS SOON AS MAN BROKE THE UNDERSTANDING OF THE FLOW, AND STARTED DOING THINGS FOR HIMSELF, HENCE HE DIED BECAUSE HE LOST HIS UNDERSTANDING, IF HE HAD KEPT IT THEN HE WOULD HAVE LIVED.

9 You have the mind to **18** take the knowledge so you may **27** have the thought of the **36** word so you may **45** understand and **54** know the **63** truth of **72** God and the **81** existence which is **90**.

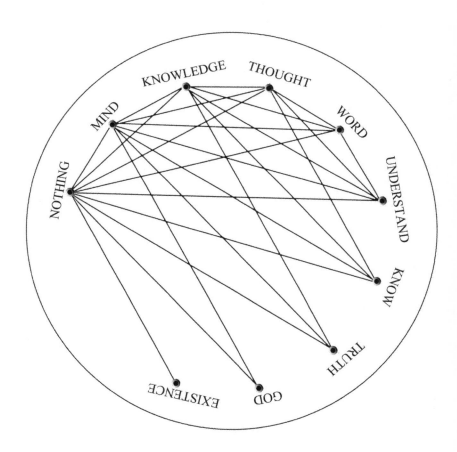

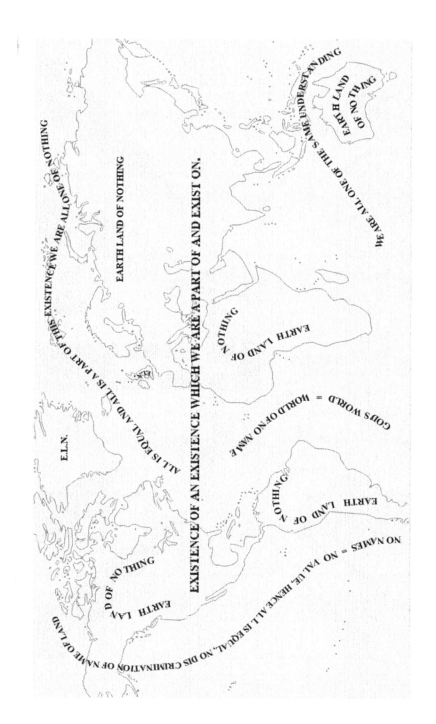

EXISTENCE OF AN EXISTENCE WHICH WE ARE A PART OF AND EXIST ON.

EARTH LAND OF NOTHING

EARTH LAND OF NOTHING

EARTH LAND OF NOTHING

EARTH LAND OF NOTHING

EARTH LAND OF NO THING

E.L.N.

GODS WORLD = WORLD OF NO NAME

WE ARE ALL ONE OF THE SAME UNDERSTANDING

OF THIS EXISTENCE WE ARE ALL ONE OF NOTHING

ALL IS EQUAL AND ALL IS A PART OF

NO NAMES = NO VALUE. HENCE ALL IS EQUAL, NO DIS CRIMINATION OF NAME OF LAND

174

WITH THE FAITH
I CARRY THE HOPE
TO FIVE AS MY CHARITY
FOR MAN TO LOVE. TO UNDERSTAND

TO KNOW
THE TRUTH
OF NOTHING
WHICH IS THE
EXISTENCE OF
GOD

THE EXISTENCE OF EVERY THING IS CREATED BY
NOTHING WHICH IS GOD.
GOD IS THE EXISTENCE OF EVERYTHING WHICH IS
NOTHING.

$G=E=N$

$E=N=G$

$N=E=G$

I PRAY WITH MY UNDERSTANDING THAN ALL MAY
KNOW YOU.

IF EVERY BODY ON THE EARTH TRULY KNEW GOD,
THEN EVERY BODY WOULD KNOW NOTHING THEN
GOD COULD DO HIS WORK AND ALL WE WOULD SEE
AND KNOW WOULD BE THE EXISTENCE.

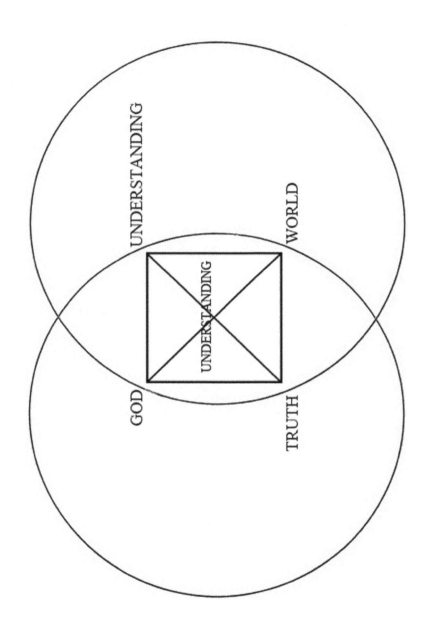

WHEN MAN WAS FIRST HERE ALL HE COULD UNDERSTAND WAS THE NINE ELEMENTS WHICH HE COULD SEE, AND COULD UNDERSTAND, THAT EACH ELEMENT MAKES THE EXISTENCE OF WHAT HE COULD SEE, WHICH WAS NOTHING.

HENCE THIS IS WHERE WE GET 0, 1, 2, 3, 4, 5, 6, 7, 8, 9

BUT HE LOST THE TRUTH

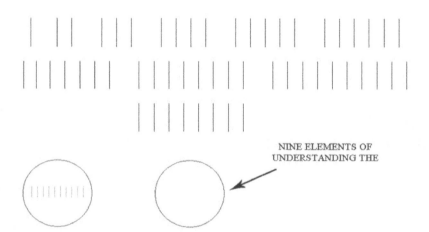

NINE ELEMENTS OF
UNDERSTANDING THE

AND THERE IS TO TRULY UNDERSTAND AND KNOW, WOULD WHAT THERE IS WITHOUT, THE WORLD WE HAVE NOW, WHICH WOULD BE THE TRUTH OF NOTHING, WHICH IS THE EXISTENCE OF GOD.

HENCE YOU WOULD UNDERSTAND HOW ALL EXISTENCES COME TO BEING AN EXISTENCE.

THE TRUE MIDDLE OF 5 = 3

THE TRUE MIDDLE OF 6 = 0

FOR THERE TO BE AN EXISTENCE OF THE MIDDLE OF 6, WHICH KEEPS AN EXISTENCE OF THE EXISTENCE = 3 – 4

WHEN YOU ASK FOR THE HALF IT IN RELATIVE TERMS YOU HAVE 3

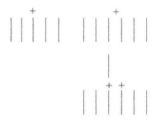

YOU TAKE THE 3 AND YOU ARE LEFT WITH AN UNBALANCE. IF YOU TAKE 3-4 THEN YOU HAVE BALANCE.

WHEN YOU HAVE HALF OF 5 YOU ARE MAKING 6. BY SPLITTING THE 3 TO ANOTHER 1, HENCE YOU MAKE A BALANCE OF 6. SO YOU SHOULD SAY LET'S SPLIT IT TO AN EQUAL BALANCE RATHER THAN SAYING "GIVE ME HALF."

$$| \; | \overset{+}{\underset{+}{|}} | \; |$$

GIVE ME HALF =

$$| \; | \overset{+}{|} | \; | - | \; | \, |+| \; | \; |$$

LET'S SPLIT TO AN EQUAL BALANCE =

$$| | + | \; | - | \; | \; | \; | | |$$

178

WHAT IS THE SOUND OF A MAN SPEAKING WITHOUT HIS TONGUE?

THE SOUND OF SILENCE.

WHAT IS THE SOUND OF A MAN PLAYING THE DRUMS WITH NO ARMS?

THE SOUND OF NOTHING.

HOW HOT IS AN UNLIT MATCH?

VERY.

HOW MANY MEN ARE TALKING WHEN THERE IS ONLY ONE MAN IN THE ROOM?

AS MANY AS HOW MANY PEOPLE ARE LISTENING?

WHAT OS TE TASTE PF WATER FROM AN EMPTY CUP?

THE SAME AS IF IT WERE FULL.

HOW COLD IS IT WHEN THE DAY IS AT ITS HOTTEST?

AS COLD AS IT IS HOT ON THE HOTTEST DAY AND AS HOT AS IT IS COLD ON THE COLDEST DAY.

WHAT CAN A BLIND MAN SEE?

AS MUCH AS HE CAN FEEL OR NOTHING THE EXISTENCE.

IF YOU ARE BLIND WHAT YOU CAN SEE IS WHAT YOU CAN SEE AT THE BACK OF *YOUR HEAD WITHOUT TURNING AROUND.*

WHAT IS HALF OF 6 = 0.

WHAT IS HALF OF 5 = 3.

WHAT IS THE EQUAL BALANCE OF 5 = 3 = 0.

WHAT IS THE EQUAL BALANCE OF 6 = 0.

HOW DO YOU MAKE THE EQUAL BALANCE OF 5 = 6.

HOW DO YOU MAKE 6 BALANCE EQUALLY = WITH THE 7TH.

WHAT IS THE EQUAL BALANCE OF ||||

WHAT IS THE OPPOSITE OF RIGHT? = IT DOES NOT EXIST.

WHAT IS TE OPPOSITE TO RIGHT?

WHAT IS THE OPPOSITE OF LEFT? WHAT IS THE OPPOSITE OF LEFT?

WHEN WAS THE UNIVERSE MADE? HOW LONG AGO?

HOW LONG WILL IT TAKE FOR THE SUN TO BURN OUT?

WHAT IS RIGHT? = NOTHING.

WHAT IS LEFT? = THE EXISTENCE OF NOTHING.

HOW MANY 9'S IN 9? = 5.

HOW MANY 3'S MAKE 3, 333? = 4.

HOW MANY CORNERS TO A SQUARE? = 8.

IF A MAN GETS HIS LEGS BIT OFF BY A LION HOW WILL HE RUN AWAY? = BY EMPTYING HIS MIND.

WHEN A MAN DECIDES TO JUMP OFF A BUILDING, WHAT IS THE FIRST THING HE MUST TAKE INTO CONSIDERATION? = MAKE SURE HE DOES NOT SURVIVE.

A MAN WHO IS WALKING AND NOT PARTICULARLY GOING ANYWHERE DECIDES TO CROSS A BRIDGE OVER A RIVER, AND CROSSING THE BRIDGE HE COMES HALF WAY AND FINDS THE OTHER HALF OF THE BRIDGE IS MISSING, WHAT WILL HE DO? = TURN BACK.

A MAN COMES UP TO YOU AND ASKS YOU FOR THE FIGURE OF TEN IN POUND COINS, HOW MANY WILL YOU GIVE HIM? 1.

A MAN IS TALKING TO YOU AND SUDDENLY STOPS TALKING – WHAT DO YOU DO? = STOP TALKING TOO.

HOW MANY CORNERS TO A CIRCLE? = (GOD KNOWS). DO NOT SPEAK, I DO NOT KNOW.

WHEN A GLASS OF WATER IS TIPPED UPSIDE DOWN, AND THEN THE RIGHT WAY UP, HOW MUCH WATER IS IN THE GLASS? = DROP.

WHEN A MAN CLIMBS TO THE TOP OF A TREE, WHERE IS HE?

A MAN STOPS YOU ON THE STREET AND ASKS YOU, "EXCUSE ME, WHERE IS MY HOME?" REPLY? = WITHIN YOURSELF.

A MAN IS ON THE PAVEMENT AND CRYING OUT FOR GOD TO HELP HIM AND SAVE HIM, "GOD, HELP ME AND GOD SAVE ME", WHAT DO YOU DO? = LEAVE HIM TO FIND GOD.

WHERE IS A DOOR WHEN NEITHER OPEN NOR CLOSED? = NOWHERE.

YOU HAVE 3 DIMENSIONS.

THE FOURTH IS WHAT PUT IT TOGETHER.

AND THE FIFTH IS THE RESULT.

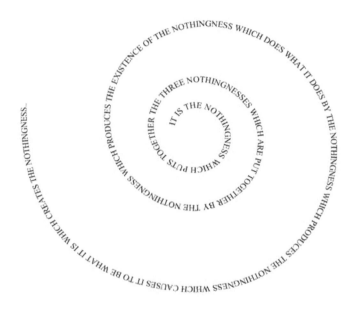

WE ARE ONLY HERE TO UNDERSTAND THE
UNDERSTANDING OF GOD.

ALL GOD WANTS IS THE UNDERSTANDING OF HIM SO WE MAY ALL BE A PART OF THE TRUTH AND TRANQUILLITY THAT LIES WITHIN US AND THE UNDERSTANDING OF TRUTH.

WHEN UTOPIA COMES ON EARTH, IT NO MORE WOULD BE AS WE KNOW IT, ONLY PEACE WITHIN OUR LORD JESUS CHRIST.

The way it should be, is the way it was, before it came to be the way it should not, and the way for it to be is not to be as it is, but to be as it is not. Then when it is not, the way it should, then it will be as it should, which, was how it was before we thought how it should be, which is why it is not, greater than what it should be. Then when it is what it was, then it will not be as it was, but how it is not. But by it not being the way it was, means that we will not know how it should be, and all we will know is how it is, rather than how it is not. So let's all try to make it the way it was and should be, rather than keeping it the way it is, which is how it should not be, which means it should be at the end as it was in the beginning so we can see the end of how it should have been, and live to an end of how it should be.

AMEN.

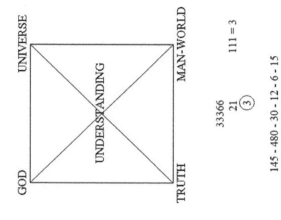

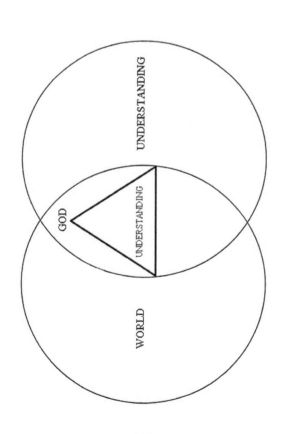

NOW AS I ONLY UNDERSTAND HUMAN BEINGS MEANS
ALL I CAN DO IS UNDERSTAND THEM.

I THINK YOU MY SWEET LORD FOR YOUR PROTECTION
FROM THE WORLD WITH THE UNDERSTANDING YOU
HAVE GIVEN UNTO ME.

I WANT FOR NO MORE
THAN TO SERVE THE PURPOSE OF
MY LORD JESUS CHRIST.

NOW I HAVE FOUND YOU I NEED ONLY TO BE WITH YOU.

WHERE IS A MAN WHEN HE IS EITHER IN OR OUT? = NOWHERE.

HOW LONG IS A PIECE OF STRING? = IT IS NOT.

HOW WAS THE UNIVERSE MADE? = THE WAY IT WAS.

WHAT IS THE SOUND OF ONE HAND CLAPPING? = NOTHING.

WHEN WILL THERE BE PEACE ON EARTH? = WHEN YOU FIND IT IN YOURSELF.

THE MEANING TO LIFE IS THERE IS NO MEANING OTHER THAN WHAT YOU CONCEIVE.

THE MEANING OF LIFE IS NO TRUTH.

THE TRUE MEANING TO LIFE IS TO KNOW GOD.

THE TRUE MEANING OF LIFE IS TO EXIST WITH GOD.

WHAT IS THE TIME? = IT IS NOW.

WHAT IS YOUR NAME? = WHAT I AM.

HOW FAR CAN A MAN RUN WITH ONE LEG? = FROM THE POINT OF WHERE HE CANNOT START.

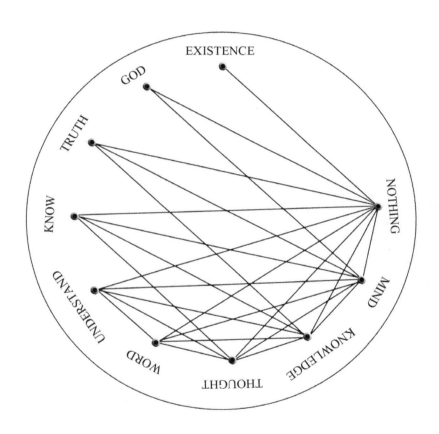

A PART OF GOD'S WORLD

7		8		9
GROWING UP WITH THE UNDERSTANDING	—	EXISTING BY THE UNDERSTANDING	—	GRACEFUL PEACE AND CONTENTMENT ON EARTH
4		5		6
UNDERSTANDING THE TRUTH	—	UNDERSTANDING GOD	—	PASSING ON THE UNDERSTANDING
1		2		3
IN THE WORLD	—	UNDERSTANDING YOUR SELF	—	UNDERSTANDING THE WORLD

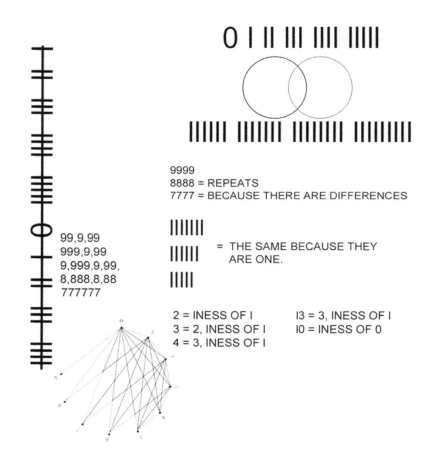

0 I II III IIII IIIII

IIIIII IIIIIII IIIIIII IIIIIIIII

9999
8888 = REPEATS
7777 = BECAUSE THERE ARE DIFFERENCES

IIIIIII
IIIIII   = THE SAME BECAUSE THEY
IIIII   ARE ONE.

99,9,99
999,9,99
9,999,9,99,
8,888,8,88
777777

2 = INESS OF I   I3 = 3, INESS OF I
3 = 2, INESS OF I   I0 = INESS OF 0
4 = 3, INESS OF I

010203040
OIOIOIOIOIOIOIOIOI
IIOI OIOIIOIIIO
II OIOIIOIII

OIOIIO
OIOIIOOIIIIOOO
OIOIIIIIOIIIIIOIIIIIIIO

OIOIIOIIIOIIIIOIIIIIOIIIIIIIOIIIIIIIIOIIIIIIIIIIO

Everything that is, is by the existence of 0 which goes up to the nine elements only of understanding.

It is understanding that all within goes back to it, and all outside it is made from it.

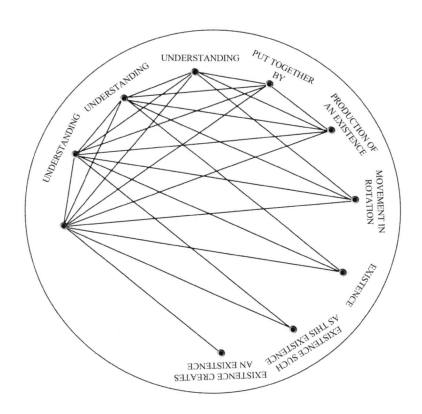

UNDERSTAND PEOPLE IN THAT WHAT EVER THEY DO IN THE WORLD AS REGARD TO WORLDLY ACTS, DO NOT KNOW GOD. UNDERSTAND THAT THEN YOU WILL UNDERSTAND YOURSELF, UNLESS YOU KNOW GOD THEN WHATEVER YOU DO IN THE WORLDS AS A PART OF THE WORLD, YOU DO NOT KNOW GOD EITHER.

ALL EXISTENCES COME FROM THE EXISTENCE OF NOTHING. ANY EXISTENCE THAT MOVES AWAY FROM THE EXISTENCE OF THE EXISTENCE OF THE EXISTENCE'S SELF, MOVES BACK TO THE EXISTENCE OF WHERE THE EXISTENCE CAME FROM, AND LEAVES ALL EXISTENCE OF NOTHING.

THE BEING OF ALL EXISTENCE THAT BECOME BEING, CAME FROM BEING NOTHING. ALL EXISTENCES THAT GO BACK TO NOTHING, BECOME BEING THE EXISTENCE OF NOTHING.

ALL EXISTENCES THAT WERE BEING THE EXISTENCES OF NOTHING WERE EXISTING AS NOTHING, THEREFORE THE NOTHINGNESS WAS BEING ALL EXISTENCE. ALL EXISTENCES THAT CAME FROM BEING NOTHING CONTINUE BEING AN EXISTENCE OF THE NOTHINGNESS THAT THE EXISTENCE WAS BEING BEFORE.

EXISTENCES COME FROM BEING NOTHING, GO TO BEING NOTHING AND GO BACK TO BEING NOTHING.

THE NOTHINGNESS PRODUCES THE 3 NOTHINGNESSES WHICH ARE PUT TOGETHER BY THE NOTHINGNESS, WHICH PRODUCES AN EXISTENCE OF NOTHING, WHICH CAUSES THE EXISTENCE OF NOTHING TO BE WHAT THE EXISTENCE IF WHICH CREATES THE EXISTENCE OF NOTHING.

ALL EXISTENCES THAT EXIST, COME FROM NOW, THERE IS NO TIME IN EXISTENCE, THERE IS ONLY NOW.
$\underline{GOD}$ = NOW
TIME

THERE IS NO LEFT IN THE WORLD, WHAT IS KNOWN AS LEFT IS ALWAYS RIGHT TO THE NEXT LEFT. THEREFORE LEFT IS THE EXISTENCE OF NOTHING, HENCE RIGHT COMES FROM NOTHING.

THE LEFT SIDE OF YOUR MIND DOES NOT EXIST, THERE IS NO LEFT, HENCE THAT IS THE EMPTY SIDE THAT

ALLOWS YOU TO PUSH YOU THE RIGHT OF THINKING AND TO ALLOW UNDERSTANDING OF THE NOTHINGNESS IN LEFT = 0 RIGHT = <u>RIGHT</u>

0

THE ELEMENTS OF UNDERSTANDING IS IN 3 UNDERSTANDINGS. I UNDERSTAND – I UNDERSTAND I UNDERSTAND – I UNDERSTAND I UNDERSTAND I UNDERSTAND. HENCE THEN YOU HAVE UNDERSTANDING. BUT YOU CAN ONLY HAVE THIS UNDERSTANDING OF TRUTHS, WHICH IS TRUTHS OF NO TRUTHS AS REGARD TO THE WORLD, AND THE TRUTH OF NOTHINGNESS. WHICH IS GOD.

THE ELEMENTS OF KNOWING ARE OF 3 – I KNOW – I KNOW THAT I KNOW – I KNOW THAT I KNOW I KNOW. BUT YOU CAN ONLY HAVE THESE KNOWINGS FIRSTLY BY KNOWING WHEN YOU DO NOT KNOW AND NOT THINKING THAT YOU KNOW, BUT BY KNOWING THAT YOU DO NOT KNOW. WHEN YOU DO NOT KNOW THEN GOD KNOWS SO LEAVE THAT TO HIM UNTIL YOU DO KNOW AND KNOW THAT YOU KNOW.

THE 3 DIMENSIONS. THERE ARE 3 DIMENSIONS, BUT IN RELATIVE TERMS THE 4 AND 5 ARE ACTUALLY BEGINNING AS 0-4 OF THE O REPRESENT THE NOTHINGNESS THAT PUTS THE THREE TOGETHER AND THE 4 BEING THE 5TH IS THE RESULT.

AN EXISTENCE WHICH IS NOT COMPOSED NATURALLY BY THE 3 ELEMENTS OF UNDERSTANDING IS NOT REAL – HENCE EVERYTHING MAN HAS MADE. ANY 3 DIMENSION THAT MAN HAS MADE, MAKES HIM THE 4TH DIMENSION = 0 – AND THE 5TH IS THE RESULT. -4.

THE EGYPTIAN PYRAMIDS WERE BUILT IN THE UNDERSTANDING THAT THE EGYPTIANS UNDERSTOOD THE EXISTENCE OF GOD. THE PYRAMIDS THEMSELVES REPRESENT HOW TO GET AND BECOME A PART OF THE

TRUTH OF GOD. THE PYRAMIDS ARE ALSO THE SPELLING OF GOD, HENCE. THE SQUARE REPRESENTS THE ELEMENTS OF UNDERSTANDING WHICH THEY HAD, WITH THE TRIANGLE IN THE SQUARE REPRESENTING THE AWARENESS IN WHERE AND HOW TO GET THE UNDERSTANDING. THE CIRCLE REPRESENTS OBEY AND BECOME A PART OF THE UNDERSTANDING, THEREFORE BACK TO THE TRIANGLE AND THAT REPRESENTS DO BY THE UNDERSTANDING, THEN WHEN YOU DO, AND EXIST BY GOD THEN YOU HAVE THE TRINITY TRIANGLE.

NOAH REPRESENTS THE ELEMENT OF RAIN. THE UNDERSTANDING OF WATER, THAT ALL EXISTENCES ARE MADE OF WATER, HENCE COME FROM WATER AND ALL EXISTENCES NEED TO DRINK WATER BECAUSE THAT'S WHERE THEY ORIGINATE FROM. NOAH'S ARK REPRESENTS THE UNDERSTANDING OF THE FLOODING OF THE EARTH. THE UNDERSTANDING OF EXISTENCES THAT WOULD COME FROM THIS ELEMENT, THE SAILING FROM THE BIBLE, THE RAIN RAINED FOR 40 DAYS, REPRESENTS THE 4TH ELEMENT FROM THE ONENESS OF THE NOTHINGNESS OF UNDERSTANDING.

ADAM AND EVE REPRESENT HOW MAN FIRST EXISTED HERE, THEY EXISTED PURELY ON UNDERSTANDING. THEY UNDERSTOOD NOTHING, HENCE EXISTED BY THE PURE FLOW OF UNDERSTANDING, HENCE GOD WAS ALLOWED TO DO HIS WORK, AND ALL THEY KNEW WAS THE EXISTENCE. THE TAKING OF THE APPLE REPRESENTS WHEN MAN FIRST DONE SOMETHING FOR HIMSELF, HENCE DONE SOMETHING OTHER THAN THE FLOW OF UNDERSTANDING, HENCE THE WORLD BEGAN THROUGH THE DISOBEDIENCE OF EXISTING. PURELY BY UNDERSTANDING, HENCE DISOBEYED GOD. JESUS REPRESENTS ALL ELEMENTS OF UNDERSTANDING, THE PURITY AND PERFECTION OF THE EXISTENCE OF NOTHING, THE ELEMENTS OF UNDERSTANDING WERE IN HIM, AND HENCE HE WAS A PART OF THE ONENESS

OF UNDERSTANDING. HE WAS THE UNDERSTANDING OF ALL, HENCE WITH THE ELEMENT HE COULD WALK ON THE SURFACE OF WATER, BECAUSE HE HAD AND WAS THE UNDERSTANDING. HE HEALED THE SICK BECAUSE HE WAS THE UNDERSTANDING OF PERFECTION OF HOW MAN WAS BEFORE THEY LOST THE EXISTENCE OF THE UNDERSTANDING OF PERFECTION IN PURITY. HENCE HE COULD PASS THE PERFECTION ON TO OTHERS BECAUSE HE WAS THE PERFECTION OF PURITY OF THE UNDERSTANDING. HENCE IF MAN HAD NOT LOST THE UNDERSTANDING, MAN WOULD HAVE EXISTED MANY MORE CENTURIES THAN HE DID. ADAM ALSO REPRESENTS THE PURITY OF EXISTENCE AND HOW LOG THE EXISTENCE OF MAN COULD HAVE EXISTED FOR, IF NOT FOR DISOBEYING THE UNDERSTANDING OF GOD, HENCE THE FLOW.

JESUS PASS ON AND SHOWED THE PERFECTION OF MAN, HENCE NO SICKNESS, WITH THE UNDERSTANDING OF GOD. THE ELEMENTS OF UNDERSTANDING, HENCE GOD, SENT THE UNDERSTANDING DOWN THROUGH JESUS FOR MAN TO TAKE THE SEED OF UNDERSTANDING THROUGH JESUS. HAD PEOPLE, THE WORLD ACCEPTED HIM AND UNDERSTOOD HIM, HENCE WOULD BE ALL NOW BE IN THE EXISTENCE OF UNDERSTANDING WITH GOD. JESUS REPRESENTS MAN AS HE TRULY IS AND NOT AS THE WORLD HAS TAUGHT HIM TO BE. HENCE JESUS IS TRUTH, THE SON OF GOD. THE SPIRIT OF JESUS WITHIN MANS TRUE SELF IS THERE WITHIN YOU, BUT UNTIL YOU SEEK.

MOSES WHO HAD UNDERSTANDING OF THE COMMANDMENTS OF GOD, THE COMMANDMENTS ARE 0-9, HENCE REPRESENTS OBEY THE NINE BECOME A PART OF THE ONENESS. THE COMMANDMENTS ARE THERE TO BE OBEYED FOR MAN TO BE WHERE HE SHOULD BE, HENCE WITHIN THE UNDERSTANDING OF GOD.

NUMBERS: WHEN MAN FIRST MARKED DOWN UNDERSTANDINGS, HENCE HE UNDERSTOOD. 0.1, THE NOTHINGNESS AND FORGIVENESS FROM THAT, THEN 0101 REPRESENTS ANOTHER ONENESS OF THE NOTHINGNESS, HENCE HE UNDERSTOOD 10101010101010101010 – ALL THE ELEMENTS OF UNDERSTANDING THAT THERE ARE TO BE UNDERSTOOD, HENCE THERE ARE NINE UNDERSTANDINGS THAT COME FROM THE ONENESS OF NOTHING. THESE UNDERSTANDS ARE WHAT MAKES THE EXISTENCE OF OUR UNIVERSE.

PERFECTION – ONLY THE PURITY OF UNDERSTANDING IS PERFECT, THERE IS NO PERFECTION IN THE WORLD OF HUMANS, HENCE THE MATERIAL WORLD. PERFECTION, HENCE ONLY WITHIN ON SELF OF UNDERSTANDING, HENCE WITH GOD.

HALFS – THE HALF OF GOD BUT THE EQUAL BALANCE IS 123, 456 HENCE 3+3 THE HALF OF 5=3. HENCE 12345 – THE EQUAL BALANCE OF 5=6 WHEN PEOPLE SAY 2½ THE HALF IS A ONE THEREFORE ½ DOES NOT EXIST OTHER THAN IN REAL TERMS OF HUMANS' FAITH, HOPE, CHARITY. FAITH MEANS ONLY TO HAVE OBEDIENCE FOR YOUR UNDERSTANDING IN GOD, HOPE TO HOPE THAT ALL WILL KNOW GOD HERE IN THIS EXISTENCE. BUT KNOWING THAT ALL SHALL KNOW GOD WHEN THEY PASS THROUGH THIS EXISTENCE TO THE NEXT. CHARITY IS YOUR UNDERSTANDING UNTO ALL THOSE WHO DO NOT KNOW GOD AND DO NOT HAVE THE FAITH. ALSO YOUR CHARITY OF THE UNDERSTANDING OF GOD IS WHAT YOU SHALL PASS ON UNTO OTHERS IN GOD'S NAME. HENCE WHEN YOU ABIDE BY THIS, THEN YOU HAVE TE TRINITY OF UNDERSTANDING.

666. REPRESENTS TWO MEANINGS, THE FIRST BEING 666 IN THE WORLD IN TERMS OF HOW FAR MAN HAS COME TO UNDERSTANDING GOD. THIS REPRESENTS 6, YOU ONLY KNOW OF THE KNOWLEDGE OF GOD. 999 REPRESENTS – 9 THE EXISTENCE OF 18 GOD OF WHICH

IS THE TRUTH YOU KNOW AND UNDERSTAND. WHEN YOU HAVE 999 AND YOU OPPOSE GOD, THEN HENCE YOU BECOME 666 AND KEEP THE WORLD AWAY FROM THE UNDERSTANDING OF GOD, WHICH YOU HAVE BUT OPPOSED. HENCE YOU ARE TRULY BAD. THE WORLD ONLY KNOWS THE KNOWLEDGE OF GOD, HENCE CHAOS FOR THE WORLD, BECAUSE THERE IS NO TRUTH IN THE HUMAN THINKING WORLD. HENCE THE WORLD GOES ON IN DECEIT OF DECEIVING EACH OTHER BECAUSE THAT'S ALL THY HAVE TO GO BY IS WHAT THE WORLD HAS TAUGHT THEM AND NOT THE TRUTH OF GOD. HENCE THE WORLD OF 666 = CHAOS.

REBORN AGAIN REPRESENTS TO BE REBORN WITH THE UNDERSTANDING OF NOTHING, HENCE AN EMPTY MIND OF THE WORLD, HENCE WITHIN THE REALM OF NOTHINGNESS AND UNDERSTANDING, HENCE REBORN IN THE SANCTUARY OF GOD. A MIND OF EMPTINESS, HENCE A MIND OF PURITY AND A HEART OF UNDERSTANDING. REBORN – OUT OF THIS WORLD OF 666 IN THE TRUTH OF GOD, I THE EXISTENCE OF NOTHING, HENCE TO KNOW NOTHING OTHER THAN THE UNDERSTANDING, GOD HAS TO GIVE UNTO YOU. FAITH IN KNOWING GOD SHALL PROVIDE ONLY UNDERSTANDING AND ONLY WHAT HE HAS TO GIVE AS IN TERMS OF ONLY WHAT YOU NEED TO EXIST WITH HIM HERE AS A PART OF THIS EXISTENCE, THE LORD IS THE SHEPHERD, YOU SHALL NOT WANT.

EXISTENCELESS = WHAT MAN HAS NEVER SEEN AND DOES NOT KNOW ABOUT. TO HIM THIS IS EXISTENCELESSNESS, WHEN MAN SEES WHAT HE HAS NEVER SEEN OR KNOWN ABOUT THEN THE EXISTENCELESS BECOMES AN EXISTENCE, EXISTENCELESS ONLY EXISTS WITH MAN, HENCE WHAT IS EXISTENCELESS TO MAN HAS ALREADY BEEN SEEN BY GOD, HENCE EXISTENCELESS EXISTS BUT DOES NOT EXIST AT ALL.

THINKING – THINKING AS THE WORLD THINKS KEEPS YOU AWAY FROM THE TRUTH AND ANY UNDERSTANDINGS THAT THERE ARE TO BE UNDERSTOOD. HENCE THE WORLD IS AS MAN HAS MADE THE WORLD, BECAUSE HE THINKS AS HE DOES. BY NOT THINKING TAKES YOU AWAY FROM HUMAN MOTION, HENCE PAIN, HAPPINESS, WANTS, AND DISLIKES, ALL OF WHICH ARE NOT REAL AND ONLY EXISTS THROUGH THINKING. JESUS DID NOT THINK, HENCE HE EXISTED PURELY ON UNDERSTANDINGS, HIS UNDERSTANDINGS WENT INTO HIS THOUGHT TO ENABLE HIM TO RELATE HIS UNDERSTANDINGS TO MAN. THE UNDERSTANDINGS CAME INTO HIS HEART WHICH WERE THEN TRANSLATED THROUGH HIS THOUGHT, HENCE THEN AS MAN THINKS. BY NOT THINKING YOU WILL EXIST ONLY WITH THE FLOW OF GOD, HENCE UNDERSTANDING WILL COME WITHIN YOU, AND YOU MAY BE CLOSE TO JESUS CHRIS. GIVE UP YOUR WORLD MEANS GIVE UP THINKING OF THE WORLD AS YOU ONCE DID. ALL MAN IS THE SAME HENCE THE THINKING SEPARATES US FROM BEING OUR TRUE SELF, HENCE MAN IS DIVIDED FROM EACH OTHER, DIVIDED FROM GOD. NOT THINKING WOULD BE THE RESULT OF ALL MAN BEING TRULY ONE WITHIN THE PALM OF GOD. HENCE PARADISE FOR ALL HERE ON EARTH UNDER THE PROTECTION IN THE SANCTUARY OF GOD.

PROSTITUTE – MEANS WOMAN WHO HAS GIVEN UP THEIR BODY FOR JESUS CHRIST, HENCE ONLY WILL THEY PASS ON THE UNDERSTANDING OF JESUS, HENCE GIVEN UP THEIR LIFE FOR GOD. HENCE WILL NEED FOR NO SEX JESUS IS THEIR LOVE. HENCE WITH THE UNDERSTANDING OF JESUS THEY SHALL PASS JESUS ONTO OTHERS, HENCE SHE IS A PROSTITUTE FOR JESUS CHRIST. SHE GIVES UNDERSTANDING ONTO OTHERS, THOSE WHO UNDERSTAND GIVE UNDERSTANDING AND LOVE BACK TO JESUS CHRIST.

REBORN – TO BE REBORN MEANS TO EMPTY YOUR MIND OF THE WORD, HENCE GO BACK TO WHEN YOU WAS BORN, HENCE KNOWING NOTHING. TO BE REBORN, HENCE TO GROW UP AGAIN IN THE UNDERSTANDING OF GOD, RATHER THAN IN THE WORLD OF HUMANS. HENCE KNOWING ONLY UNDERSTANDING OF TRUTH RATHER THAN THE HUMAN WORLD OF DECEIT. REBORN – TO HAVE NO HUMAN EMOTION ONLY TO HAVE UNDERSTANDING OF HUMANS. BUT NOT BE AS THEY ARE WITHIN YOU. REBORN TO UNDO ALL THE WORLD HAS TAUGHT YOU, HENCE NO THINKING ONLY WHAT GOD HAS TO GIVE. HENCE SACRIFICE YOUR WORLD FOR GOD, FOR TRUTH OF UNDERSTANDING, HENCE THINK OF THE WORLD NO MORE, ONLY UNDERSTANDING OF THE WORLD. REBORN HENCE CONTINUE YOUR LIFE IN THE WORLD AS TRULY HUMAN. HENCE SACRIFICE OF ALL PAST WORLDLY FRIENDS. HENCE WITH THEM WILL BE NO LIFE SA THEY WORLD REMAINS. HENCE YOUR FRIENDS OF THE PAST WILL LEAVE YOU BECAUSE THEY GIVE THEM ONLY TRUTH. HENCE ONLY THOSE WHO WANT YOUR UNDERSTANDING WILL STAY.

LIGHT -= NOTHINGNESS TRAVELS FASTER THAN THE SPEED OF LIGHT. NOTHINGS IS SPEED OF A NATURE THAT CAN NOT BE SEEN OTHER THAN IN THE EXISTENCE THAT THE NOTHINGNESS PRODUCES. THE SPEED OF NOTHINGNESS CAN NOT BE MEASURED IN ANY WAY OR FORM. HENCE THIS IS SPEED WITHOUT SPEED. NOTHINGNESS CAN NOT BE SEEN AS NOTHING, AS NOTHING IS ALWAYS WITH YOU, HENCE THIS MAY BE SEEN BEFORE ANY LIGHT. $\underline{SPEED} = \underline{NOTHINGNESS}$
$$\frac{SPEED}{LIGHT} = \frac{NOTHINGNESS}{FASTER}$$

GOD, GOD IS ALL, HENCE ALL THAT IS THE UNIVERSE, HENCE ALL EXISTENCES OF EVERY EXISTENCE. GOD – ALL ELEMENTS OF UNDERSTANDING WHICH CREATE ALL EXISTENCES. HENCE SUNS, PLANETS, GOD – ALL

FEATURES OF LIGHT, ALL FEATURES OF SPEED AND HAPPINESS WITHIN THE UNIVERSE. GOD IS THE EXISTENCE OF NOTHING, HENCE NOTHINGNESS. ALL EXISTENCES COME FROM WITHIN THE NOTHINGNESS, HENCE UNDERSTANDING FROM GOD. GOD ALWAYS BEING NOTHINGNESS ALWAYS BEING AS NOTHING. HENCE GOD IS NOW ALWAYS WITH MAN, GOD IS HERE TO BE UNDERSTOOD THROUGH THE NOTHINGNESS. GOD IS LOVE OF UNDERSTANDING, FORGIVENESS AND INNER WARMTH. MAN IS A PART OF THE UNIVERSE, HENCE IS A PART OF GOD, BUT IS DISTANT FROM GOD UNTIL GOOD IS UNDERSTOOD. GOD REPRESENTS ALL EXISTENCES WHICH ARE COMPOSED ONLY BY THE ELEMENT OF UNDERSTANDING. GOD, MAKER OF ALL THAT IS GOD IS GOOD. ALL UNDERSTANDINGS CREATE EXISTENCES ONLY BY UNDERSTANDING, HENCE ALL THAT IS COMPOSED BY THE NOTHINGNESS RETURNS BACK TO THE NOTHINGNESS. EXISTENCES ONLY PRODUCE EXISTENCES, HENCE THERE IS NO END, ONLY BEGINNINGS OF EXISTENCES, WHICH ARE ALWAYS BEING. KNOWINGS AND FAITH. GOD – NO DEATH JUST THE BEING OF ONE EXISTENCE PASSING THROUGH TO BEING THE NEXT. GOD – GIVE YOUR LIFE TO GOD, HENCE EXIST WITHIN HIS SANCTUARY. GOD – NEVER STARTED, ALWAYS HAS BEEN, ALWAYS SHALL CONTINUE BEING. HENCE ALL GOES BACK TO GOD FROM WHENCE THEY CAME. HENCE FROM THE EXISTENCE OF NOTHINGNESS TO BEING AN EXISTENCE OF NOTHING BACK TO BEING NOTHINGNESS. GOD – UNDERSTANDING WITHIN EXISTENCES OF UNDERSTANDINGS, HENCE ELEMENTS OF UNDERSTANDING. GOD – REPRESENTS 9 – HENCE THE NINE UNDERSTANDINGS WHICH CAME FROM GOD, HENCE NOTHINGNESS, AND PRODUCES THE EXISTENCE OF GOD. HENCE THE ENTIRE UNIVERSE. GOD'S UNDERSTANDINGS PUT TOGETHER PRODUCE ONE ELEMENT OF EXISTENCE. HENCE THE

UNDERSTANDINGS GO UP TO NINE UNDERSTANDINGS WHICH IS THE ULTIMATE OF UNDERSTANDINGS. AND AS A RESULT, TOUCHING A SOLID EXISTENCE OF WHICH ALL OTHER ELEMENTS OF EXISTENCES COME FROM. THREE UNDERSTANDINGS COME FROM UNDERSTANDING, TURN INTO NINE UNDERSTANDINGS AND ALL OTHER EXISTENCES OF UNDERSTANDINGS COME FROM WITHIN THIS, HENCE THE PROOF OF GOD.

Get rid of all that the world gave you.

Empty yourself out of mind and feelings. Be empty.

Receive only what God has to give you.

It is a known truth, exp, if I am well I will come and see you. Now you may say if I am well I will come and see you, but in fact you may be well and not go at all. Therefore, if you are confident of what is really happening, hence cover up of truth or not certain what to do. It may be if I leave at 2 o'clock I shall be down to you at 5 o'clock but maybe lots of traffic and flat tyre, so the truth is it's well possible at 2 o'clock I could leave here and be down to you when I get there.

To say if I leave at 2 o'clock I will be down to you at 5 o'clock, but maybe you leave at 2 and a flat tyre comes and you did not say, if I leave at 2 and be down at 3, but maybe you will be held in traffic, then you did not say if I leave at 2, if I have a flat, if I do not get held in traffic. So because there are so many technicalities you should say, well, I shall leave at 2 or thereabouts, and be down to you when I can.

HAVE LOVE SO YOU MAY GIVE IT.

HAVE FAITH SO YOU MAY SHARE IT.

HAVE CHARITY SO YOU MAY BE CHARITABLE.

HAVE HOPE SO YOU MAY HOPE ALL WILL KNOW GOD.

HAVE CONTENTMENT SO YOU MAY BE CONTENT.

HAVE GRACE SO YOU MAY BE GRACEFUL.

HAVE SELFLESSNESS SO YOU MAY BE SELFLESS.

HAVE RESPECT SO YOU MAY GIVE IT.

HAVE INNER STRENGTH SO YOU MAY KEEP IT FOR GOD.

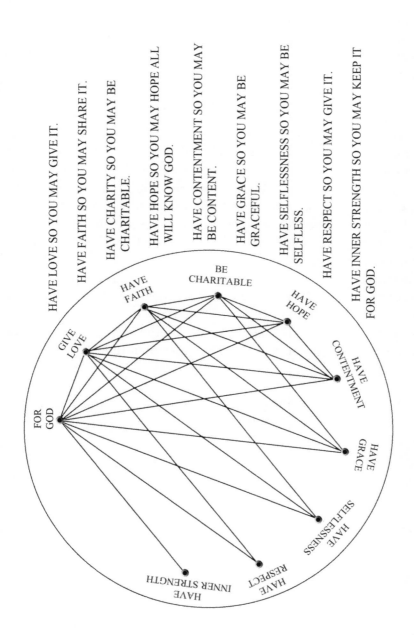

A man is standing on a street corner, admiring the stars. Then a lady came up to him and asked if she could be of any service to him. He answered, "Can you teach me of Jesus Christ." She replied, "No, I cannot." Then he said "Then you can be of no service to anyone."

The OK Man

There was a man who lived in China and for many years he was a messenger for people. He would ride a bike on walk depending on the demand of how long he had to go and how many people needed messages sent. He had done this job for many years and was quite popular with the people of his town. One day when riding his bike, he felt a cramp in both of his legs. It forced him to call of the bike. Later when he was found and taken home, a doctor came and told him he would never walk again. When all his friends came round to see him, they were all upset about his misfortune, this man, and when they asked him how he was, he just smiled and said "I'm OK." There were two men who were out walking on day, and one man said to the other, "What is the distance between and you I?" The other man replied, "Whatever you think."

TELEVISION =   POLLUTION
                 BAD SPIRITS

56
30
11
92=11=2

107=8
CONNECTION

97
10
7

TWO MEN ARE WALKING TOGETHER, ONE MAN IS CALLED GOT EVERYTHING IN THE WORLD, AND THE OTHER IS CALLED HAS NOTHING. GOT EVERYTHING IN THE WORLD SAYS TO HAS NOTHING, "TELL ME OF ALL YOU HAVE IN THE WORLD, AND TELL ME OF YOUR PAST." HAS NOTHING REPLIED, "I HAVE ONLY NOW."

A MAN IS SITTING BY A RIVER, HIS NAME IS CLEAR MIND. WHEN APPROACHED HIM CAME A MAN AND SET BESIDE HIM. THEY TOGETHER FOR SOME TIME, WHEN THE MAN WHO JOINED CLEAR MIND PULLED OUT FROM HIS POCKET A BOTTLE, THIS WAS A BOTTLE OF SPIRIT ALCOHOL. THE MAN ASKED CLEAR MIND, "WOULD YOU LIKE TO SHARE THIS BOTTLE OF ALCOHOL WITH ME?" CLEAR MIND REPLIED, "NO THANK YOU I HAVE MYSELF ALREADY."

A MAN WAS IN A PARK, HE WAS SHOUTING AND SWEARING IN A BITTER WAY AND GETTING TO BE QUITE ANGRY WITH HIMSELF. WHEN UP TO HIM CAME A LITTLE CHILD OF UNDER 6 AND ASKED "EXCUSE ME MISTER WHAT IS IT LIKE TO BE YOUR AGE?" THE MAN CALMED DOWN AND HE SAID "IF I HAD ANY SENSE I WOULD BE YOUR AGE AGAIN."

THERE WAS A WOMAN IN A HOSPITAL AND TO PEOPLE SHE WAS KNOWN TO BE SENILE. SHE DID NOT THINK AT ALL ABOUT ANYTHING. SHE WAS ALWAYS HAPPY SHE HAD NO PROBLEMS WITH HER SELF. SHE ALWAYS SMILED IN ANY SITUATION, BUT WITH THIS SHE WAS ALWAYS VERY HELPFUL... NOW IN THE HOSPITAL THERE WORKED A PORTER, AND UP UNTIL THIS TIME HE WAS ALWAYS IN A MOOD, NEVER THE SAME FROM ONE DAY TO THE NEXT... HE HAD A TEMPER HE UPS AND DOWNS THE LOT, WHEN ONE DAY HE MET UP WITH THE LADY, IN DOING SO HE ASKED HER, "EXCUSE ME MAM WHAT ARE YOU THINKING?" SHE REPLIED "NOTHING." HE SAID AFTER "I UNDERSTAND."

I DRINK TO MAKE THE DAY GO FASTER
I DRINK TO DROWN THE SORROWS
I DRINK TO FORGET THE WORLD
I DRINK TO BE MERRY
I DRINK TO BE DRUNK
I DRINK BECAUSE JESUS DID
I, WHAT DO YOU SUPPOSE JESUS WOULD HAVE
DRANK FOR

YYYY   BIHHII JAKEYYYYYYYYYYY   OPOO U U U U

OOOO O O O L L L L L L O PPPP P P P & & £ & (£""""

H HH & HELLO   EXISTENCE

EXISTENCE $ I U

MONEY	=	give to your MASTER awareness and OBEDIENCE to the NOTHINGNESS and the EXISTENCE of kindness when gives you to YONDER.
IN REPLY	=	thank you.
HUMAN	=	lack of HONESTY and UNDERSTANDING to your MASTER and not being AWARE of the NOTHINGNESS.
HUMAN	=	HONESTY and UNDERSTANDING of your MASTER of the AWARENESS of NOTHING.
PROPHET	=	the PEOPLE with RESPECT to the OBEDIENCE, who PERFORM unto others the HONESTY of EXISTENCE and the TRUTH of god.
SAINT	=	SANCTUARY in the AWARENESS of god as one a part of the oneness with the existence of the NOTHINGESS and the TRUTH.
DEATH	=	DISCIPLE disobeying the EXISTENCE = the AWARENESS, the TRUTH and HONESTY.
LIFE	=	LOVE the ONE and ONENESS, the FATHER of EXISTENCE.
KEY	=	KINDNESS to the EXISTENCE of YONDER.
NOAH	=	the existence of NOTHING as one of the elements of understanding OBEYING the AWARENESS of creation and the HONESTY of god's sanctuary.
ARK	=	AWARENESS and RESPECT of the KINDNESS from god.
SON	=	SANCTUARY in the OBEDIENCE of the NOTHINGNESS.
WOW	=	become aware of the WARENESS and be OBEDIENT to WARENESS you have become aware of.

AND	=	AWARENESS of NOTHING DISOBEYED.
GOD	=	to GOD be OBEDIENT.
SURE	=	SANCTUARY in the UNDERSTANDING by giving RESPECT to the EXISTENCE.
HELP	=	be HONEST to the understanding of the EXISTENCE give LOVE to all PEOPLE in need.
FIRE	=	to the FATHER of the ONENESS give RESPECT to his EXISTENCE.
EAT	=	EXIST only on the AWARENESS of TRUTH.
FOOD	=	to my FATHER I OBEY with OBEDIENCE as his DISCIPLE.
GOT	=	to GOD, OBEY his TRUTH.
WHAT	=	WARENESS, HONESTY of the AWARENESS of TRUTH.
WAS	=	WARE of the awareness got ABUSED and is now SANCTIONED by God.
S	=	SANCTUARY and SPREAD the word.
W	=	WARENESS where chosen to use the earth as understanding
E	=	EXISTENCE and the
J	=	UNDERSTANDING of the ONE as a part of the ONENESS of the
BLESS	=	may you BECOME a part of the LOVE for the EXISTENCE in the SANCTUARY of the SANCTUARY of God.
BLISS	=	to BECOME a part of the love and the ONENESS in the SANCTUARY of the SANCTUARY of the EXISTENCE of nothing.
HATE	=	to have no HONESTY or obedience to the AWARENESS and have no TRUTH, and go against the EXISTENCE of you.

210

HOW	=	HONESTY OBEY the WARENESS.
WHO	=	WARENESS of HONESTY OBEYED.
FINE	=	FATHER of the ONENESS of the NOTHINGNESS of the EXISTENCE.

UNDERSTOOD

D	=	DISCIPLE of God.
O	=	OBEDIENT to as a
O	=	OBEY and are
T	=	TIME of which you
S	=	SANCTUARY in God's
R	=	RESPECT and take
E	=	EXISTENCE of which you
D	=	DISCIPLE you are of the
N	=	NOTHING
U	=	UNDER

UNDERSTANDING

G	=	GOD
N	=	NOTHINGNESS of the existence of
I	=	one of the ONENESS in the
D	=	DISCIPLE as part of the
N	=	NOTHINGNESS as a
A	=	AWARENESS of the
T	=	TIME
S	=	SANCTUARY in God's
R	=	RESPECT and take
E	=	EXISTENCE of which you
D	=	DISCIPLE you are of the
N	=	NOTHING
U	=	UNDER
IN	=	you are one a part of the ONENESS of NOTHING.
OUT	=	become a part of the OBEDIENCE and UNDERSTANDING of the TRUTH.

W	=	WARENESS
O	=	OBEY the last of the
R	=	PEOPLE but do not
R	=	RESPECT the worlds
O	=	OBEY the awareness
B	=	BE aware of the awareness

H	=	HONESTY
S	=	SANCTUARY of the
U	=	UNDERSTANDING
H	=	HOUR of the
S	=	SILENCE of the

HOPE = HONESTY OBEDIENCE and respect for the existence

= honest and obedient to the respect that all people shall know the existence of God.

LOVE = LIFE by the existence of God. OBEYED by the understanding pass on to all VISITORS of EXISTENCE.

FAITH = FATHER of the AWARENESS of the ONENESS of the TRUTH of the Holy Spirit.

STEAL = SANCTUARY in God's TIME, EXISTENCE and ABUSING the LOVE.

BEG = BEDIENCE for the EXISTENCE of GOD.

SORRY = SANCTUARY in the OBEDIENCE in RESPECTING PEOPLE of YONDER.

THANK = In God's TIME I understand the HONESTY and the AWARENESS of NOTHING and the KINDNESS I receive.

KNOW	=	KINDNESS given to the NOTHINGNESS OBEYING the WARENESS.
KILL	=	The KINDNESS has now gone from existence that was in you.
	=	the one of the ONENESS. LACK of LOVE unto others.
DANGER	=	DUE to the AWARENESS of NOTHING which is GOD the EXISTENCE and have RESPECT.
WARNING	=	be WARE of the AWARENESS. Do not give lack of RESPECT to the NOTHINGNESS as you are a part of one of the ONENESS of the NOTHINGNESS of GOD.
TO	=	TRUTHFUL OBEDIENCE

RUSSIA WOULD FALL / CONVERSION OF RUSSIA

VIRGIN MARY (CHRIST)?

CAME TO 3 GIRLS = SISTERS AND SAID ① CONVERSION
OF RUSSIA WOULD FALL

②

③

...

ALL THOSE WHO PASSED THROUGH IN THE WORLD
WITH THE TORMENTED SPIRIT OF THE WORLD GOES
BACK FRO WHERE THE SPIRIT CAME FROM. THAT SPIRIT
IS NOT ALLOWED BACK BECAUSE JESUS CHRIST'S SPIRIT
IS HERE FOR THEM. ALL THOSE WHO PASS THROUGH
THIS WORLD WITH THE SPIRIT OF GOD WITHIN THEM,
STAY SO THEY MAY BE PASSED ON WITH JESUS CHRIST.

1. RUSSIA WOULD FALL – HAS FALLEN.
2. 2. AMERICA BY ALL ARMS – BECOMES STRONG
   IN WORLD POWER.
3. RUSSIA BECOMES ECONOMICAL –
4. TURN CHRISTIAN?

GOOD FOR SOME   ⟶   FOR THOSE WHO KNOW
JESUS CHRIST

BAD FOR OTHERS   ⟶   FOR THOSE WHO DO NOT.

<u>1917</u> = <u>36 </u> = 9

JESUS <u>13</u>TH

46			49			3
	35		38		15	
		33	30	27		
2	12	20	25	31	37	48
		32	19	18		
	36		13		14	
47			1			4

46	48	
35	37	15
33	31	21
25	25	25
22	20	32
14	12	36
4	2	43
179	175	172

To be reborn means to know what you knew as a baby and to exist. This understanding of no thinking of God. Then once you do this, then you will know only truths. And become a disciple of God and the way you do this is to stop thinking as you do the world has taught you, and stop relating to the world and start knowing the nothingness and what all existences are. Being reborn in society is difficult because of the social demand by others, and the demand you have for yourself. You have to first give up your circle of life to enable you to be part of the nothingness of God. This takes immeasurable understanding to achieve. Do this and you shall be in the realm of God, and all his understandings. You must have respect, loyalty and obedience of your master maybe to stay in his sanctuary. The closer you become to him, the closer you are to being what you truly are and not as the world has made you.

REBORN   =   SANCTUARY
NOTHINGNESS   GOD

The fact God is always with you but now he is in you and he is not within you. God is there for all, and only by giving up yourself for him and by not thinking as the world has taught you keep out the spirits that try to come in the mind to your right, keep them out with the nothingness in your left. This changes understanding rather than thinking what is true keeping you away from the truth fight it, keep it out, hence peace shall prevail. God is only understanding, he cannot be in you until you are in him. Then you will be part of the others what you truly are. Then may you walk with Jesus Christ, away from the world.

LIFE   = CONFUSION = EXISTENCE =   CONTENT
WORLD   CHAOS   GOD   UNDERSTANDING

Have only understanding of the world then you can understand that people do what they do and why. Hence with your understanding you will speak only the truth, before you know and know that you know there you are not thinking, you just know in your understanding.

216

You will never know anything by writing about whatever you want to know. When you do not know, then know you do not know, yet do know. Let the thinking side of whatever it was you wanted to know and stop thinking.

Nothing changes all the time. To say nothing changes is truth, but not in the context that this is said. Because every existence is nothing and has to change from one existence to another, therefore nothing always changes. But to say "Nothing changes around here" in the context of "This is still what this was and will not change" is wrong. Therefore, nothing changes and nothing always will. To say "Nothing changes with you" is to say. "You are still what you are and what you were, and there will be no difference." This is non truth, because however you are now, you will change, hence yes "Nothing changes with you." To say "Nothing changed around here" in the context that this is used is non truth because you are saying that everything is still the same. But in fact, nothing's changing all the time, so to say "Nothing's changed around here" is truth. When you ask someone, "What did you do today?" When they reply "Nothing," this is fact so then you would reply "Good you're speaking the truth."

When you say "Nothing is happening here," in the context of "There's nothing going on" this is non truth because nothing is always happening and always going to. So "nothing is happening here" is truth. But not in the context that this is used. To say "I won nothing at Bingo is non truth" because you cannot win nothing. But to say "I did not win anything" is truth. To say "I won no-thing at bingo" is truth. To say "Nothing's wrong" is non truth because nothing's right therefore nothing is not right or wrong. To say "No-thing's wrong" is wrong because there are no-things that are right. Therefore everything is wrong. Because there is only nothing, therefore nothing is right, to say "Nothing is right" is non truth. Because nothing is not wrong. Nothing just nothing, therefore this is right, but not in the context of everything is not going as everything should. To say "No-thing-is right" is right, because there is nothing that is right, to say "No-thing-is wrong" is wrong, because there is no-thing that is right for a wrong to come from, but everything is wrong then.

Once you know God, then you have faith, because in the beginning you must have had belief of God, but then he showed himself to you, so once he has done this then when people ask you do you belief in God, you will answer "No, I have faith." To say you believe means that you have not seen and can only believe. To say you have faith means whatever you believed in has shown itself to you. Then you when reply, "I have faith in God," they will want to know why, or how. But when you say you believe in God, then of course they have not seen God then they will reply that they do not believe because they have not seen. The only believe you may have without seeing for yourself, as in God, there is nothing in the world worth the thought of belief. As God exists, and is around all the time, then you may only have belief in God. Then as you understand God the belief goes, and you have faith, etc. "I HAVE FAITH IN GOD."

Have no belief in <u>no-thing</u>.

Have faith in <u>nothing.</u>

To have faith in nothing, is to have faith in <u>no-things.</u>

I believe in no-thing.

I have faith in nothing.

No-thing is worth the thought of belief.

To have faith in nothing is to be truly sane.

To have faith in things is madness.

To have faith in God is to have faith in no-thing.

Daytime proves to us the existence of light and the existence of nothing. Night proves to us the existence of all existences plus the existence of light, but night does not prove to us the existence of darkness, hence darkness does not exist within the universe, there is only light.

When Jesus drank wine, this was wine of zero content of alcohol. He did not require any thing from alcohol as humans in the world need. He had already the joy and understanding of God. He needed no alcohol to put him on another way of being, hence to drown his sorrow. Jesus was perfect and did not reach this intake as man does.

Stone Henge is an understanding of what man had of God. This represents where the sun and moon was. Stone Henge is the centre point of this understanding. The outer circle represents the sun, the inner represents the moon, and the U-shape in the middle is the sign that they understood the centre point of this understanding. From this centre point, more understanding could come to them of the movement of God. Hence this was the centre point for understanding of the existence of God. Hence sun-moon-direction. This place was burnt out for the purity of understanding, not as a use to man as a calendar. By understanding these understandings, this gave them, from God, an understanding of him as the existence of all existences. Hence, only to be closer to him, in understanding what he does. But these understandings were not for man's use, only to be closer to their creator.

Calendars should not exist, for they remind you of the past which you should not have, and the future which is not yours to plan for.

The existence of nothingness is faster than the speed of light. Hence the nothingness turns the universe around, nothing-ness is always there before light. The nothingness is able to turn the universe around with all existence within the nothingness turning as well. The speed of nothingness is speed to the very limit of speed. This is a speed that man will never be able to get to. Hence as soon as he tries to make something go faster than the speed of light, this will turn into nothing. Which means this will already be nothing, before it reaches anywhere near the speed of nothingness. The nothingness is a speed which has no speed, this speed cannot be measured or timed. This is the forge which turns the whole of the existence of all the existences around. Although this speed cannot be seen, there is no edge of the force, hence you can always travel through the galaxies without being stopped by the force. The nothingness can neither be felt, has a speed or be sampled. Nothingness travels through every existence. Light cannot do this. Nothingness does. The 3 understandings that make the first existence of an existence come from this speed and when the 3 come together, the speed at which they were brought together is such that a result of this understanding comes. Hence with the flow of the force, this understanding goes round and round, hence it is the beginning of an existence.

SPEED   =   NOTHINGNESS
LIGHT   FASTER

11

100 X TOTAL POWER PLUS

LIGHT

In terms of man stating "Nothing goes faster than the speed of light." Hence this is truth with the understanding of nothingness.

Nothingness is to you before the existence of any light through the speed of nothingness. Hence all existences came. Light is the result from the speed of the nothingness. The speed of nothingness is only visible in that which the nothingness produces and that which the nothingness does, hence rotate. Other than this there is no proof in physical terms of measurement and feeling the nothingness is always with you and needs no outside existence to help the motion of what the nothingness does. Light needs help from the nothingness and the speed in which the nothingness travels in order to produce the motion which makes the existence of light.

SPEED = NOTHINGNESS = SPEED = LIGHT

NOTHINGNESS = LIGHT

I understand that, that that surrounds me, I exist as a part of that which exists, which is the surroundings that I know have not been thought of but is a result of understanding. Therefore, I understand, I exist as a part of understanding. Through my understanding, I am aware of my existence by the reflection of water and all the existences of understanding. I exist without the mind to recognise that I am, my understanding allows me to be aware of y existence through the awareness of my true surroundings. I understand the existence of other existences, therefore I exist as a part of existences before I had the mind to think. My thinking is my distracter from understanding of truth. My thinking is my enemy of God and his understanding that he has to share with me. Therefore I exist as an existence of and as a part of all existences, without any thought or think. Emptiness of my mind, through this gives me the understanding of truth, that I exist as one, with the oneness of all existences of understanding and not as a part of that that I think, or that that has been thought of.

I am free from doubt, my understanding is truth given unto me from God. I have no reason to doubt what I do not know. I understand that I do not know so therefore I have no doubt in my mind or hart. I do not know there for god knows

Finally, I know God has given unto me a blessing of understanding. I do not create an idea that I know for that is straying from God. I wait until he allows me to know and would memorise and lay in the bliss of knowing nothing. And I have the knowing that I do not know, and what I obey.

There is no Noah's Ark. The earth was flooded as part of one of the elements of understanding but when water covers as parts of elements the existence of water creates an existence. Water is part of the oneness of elements that produces the existence of the existence that is here now. Water is the 4th element of understanding which creates the existence of other understanding. Water element what happened as a result of much rain in the beginning and the result of that element of understanding, created oceans and hence an existence from that. God is the creator of existences hence he does not create man's material world as the Bible says, destroy. There is no Ark in Turkey.

There is no Noah's Ark. The earth was flooded as part of one of the elements of understanding that went the existence of water comes as part of one existence, hence the existence of water creates an existences. Water is part of the oneness of elements that produce the existence of other understandings. Noah represents what happened as a result of mass raisin, in the beginning. And the result of that understanding created oceans and hence all existences that come from that element. God is the creator of existences, hence he does not create them purposely as the Bible says to destroy. By the Bible saying that Noah was ordered to build an ark and collect animals, because he was going to destroy the earth is saying that God purposely did that. To purposely destroy is a human act, and not the act of God. God is the creator of existences and of understanding which just does what it does through the flow and does not plan destruction of God.

Man through his thinking and ideas has destroyed for himself the understanding of God. Now he just creates pictures of the truth but in an untruthful way. The Bible is there to be understood, not read with the thinking side of you which is the right side, but to be understood with the left side. So you all want the true meanings behind what the Bible says about God. The Bible is called the truth by some, and not the truth by others. The ones who say the Bible is true are correct in an incorrect way. The ones who say the Bible is not true are not correct but in a correct way. So the Bible is true in an incorrect way. The closer you are to the Bible, in a way that it's actually the further you are away from God, the closer you are to the Bible in understanding what the Bible represents, the closer you are in understanding God.

EXISTENCE = 0
   GOD

Jesus walked on water because he had the understanding of the elements of air. He healed the sick because he had the purity and perfection of understanding by him being the elements. Jesus Christ was perfect in understanding all. This is the only perfection there is. There is no worldly perfection in all of man's creation.

UNDERSTANDING   =   JESUS CHRIST
   PERFECTION   THE EXISTENCE OF GOD

JESUS =   10
            1 A PART OF THE ONENESS AS ONE

Man has the understanding of what to obey, which is not to obey man or human.

The 10 commandments' represent, obey the 9 to become a part of the oneness of God.

9 COMMANDMENTS   =   1 UNDERSTANDING

TO BECOME A PART OF   =   EXISTENCE OF GOD

The existence or exists when you see an existence, an existence only exists as an existence if being seen before you saw the existence, but if not for anyone seeing an existence, then it is existence less to us. An existence is existence less before we see the existence. An existence exists because we can see the existence, therefore we can the existence exists if looked at, then after the existence has been seen then you have an existence, but before that of the existence, then the existence is existence less. What you cannot see which has not been seen is existence less to you, the existence of an existence if nothing, but the existence less is nothing at all hence nothingness. The existence less does not existent as an existence. The existent less goes beyond the nothingness, because the existence does not exist at all. Before the existent less has been seen by any man, but when you see the existent less than an existence comes from the existent less and exists as a nothing and as a part of the nothingness. The existence of nothing exists when you see what exists, and is an existence before you or any man saw it, because what man has never seen to him it is existent less, but your existent less has already been seen by God, so it exists as an existence by the eye of the three elements of understanding of how to do things.

The first time you do something, if it fails then when it comes to the second time, you must understand that your ego must not be there and be tempted to do whatever it is. Then you must realise your own physical actions and try another way. If this fails, then you must have nothing to do with it, both in action and mind. And understand that it is nothing, and not worth the thought of it. And you must just know and know that you know what it is that you have to do then you will get it.

3RD TIME LUCKY
UNDERSTANDING

The 3 elements of understanding of doing things.

1. Understand what it is you have to do.
2. Understand how you are going to do it, by not thinking about it and by letting the flow of understanding take control.
3. Understand the 2 and just do it.

1. Understanding what it is you have to do.
2. Understanding how you are going to do it.
3. Just doing it.

$$\frac{3}{\text{UNDERSTANDING}} \quad = \quad \frac{\text{EXISTENCE}}{0} \quad = \quad \text{GOD}$$

Finally,

> Once all levels of understanding are known on all three levels, then you must find the inner strength to cope with all the responsibility of knowing God, and the burden is high upon the conscience when God is not obeyed. Also you must cope with the knowing that the true beauty of people has been lost to the selfish course of humanity. Then finally once you know and understand of the purity then

> One must cope with the realisation that also

> One is with God, that also

> One is very much alone

> And to enlighten

> One person is to save the whole of humanity to

> One being and to be not a part and

> One with God for the

> One goal of the unselfish good of mankind to be

> One strength of a great to a greater

> One unity of grave and anguishlessness to be

> One with the universe of purity =

You can push out your thinking from the right by not thinking from the left. Hence understanding will be allowed to filter through the left side of your mind which is the right side. By the left side taken in the understanding you are able to keep and understand more, by keeping away the right. The world comes in on the right. The elements of understanding come in on the left. The left will keep the right away, with faith.

MIND DIRECTION   MIND DIRECTION

LEFT =   RIGHT   =   RIGHT   =   WRONG

Nothing is right to say something is right is wrong because there is only nothing to be right about. To say turn right is wrong because there is no left to turn right into. To say turn left is to say turn right into nothing.

| $\underline{\text{LEFT}}$ | = | $\underline{\text{RIGHT}}$ | - | $\underline{\text{RIGHT}}$ | = | $\underline{\text{RIGHT}}$ |
| LEFT | | 0 | | RIGHT | | 0 |

When you have left and you put something to the left then the left becomes right which means the left was nothing.

When you have right and you put something to the right the right remains right of nothing.

LEFT = 0

RIGHT = $\underline{\text{RIGHT}}$ - There is no right in the world, there is only left.
$\quad\quad\quad\quad$ 0

The left side of your mind is nothing which means everything is to your right.

But every truth is to your left which = 0.

There is no right in things.

There is only right in nothing.

The existence of nothing is right.

The existence of something is wrong.

What right do we have to put a right to nothing?

What right do we have to say something is right when the truth is nothing is right

The existence of this planet was made on the 7th element of understanding. As there is no time means that the existence was created in no time, which is now. God's time is now, and now only. Therefore the existence of this existence is possible for the time to have been 7 days in the most impossible way. You can say one minute or one hour, because as there is no time, hence possible in the impossible way. The existences can come from how they happened. Now is God's time, which could have been the making of the existence one second ago, but the fact is the existence was made now.

GOD = TIME
NOW

The right side of your mind is the left side and it is right.

The right side of your mind is right but is not right and is wrong.

The left side of your mind is in the middle of the right and is the right truth. The left side of your mind is nothing and holds the truth. The right side takes in the world of thinking and overpowers the left. All worldly thoughts that come in from the right can be pushed out by the existence of nothing from the left. Left has no opposite of left but right has an opposite of right, which is wrong. Hence from the left of your mind allows you true understanding of truths. But what the right takes in it cannot understand hence confusion of spirits. The left is the open existence of nothing for to understand all truths in existence because there is nothing to interfere with the understanding element of you. But the right interferes with the left because that part thinks and feels trapped, hence keeps you away from understanding. But master the left and understanding of God shall come.

The Bible is the only way man in his present state can see God. But the Bible lies, only because if it told the real truth then we would now be with truth. But because man went wrong and lost his understanding of the way things truly are, hence he wrote the Bible to the mind of man, and not to mind of understanding. You will read about Adam and Eve. They never existed. Adam and Eve in the form that the Bible says. Adam and Eve represents the mankind that had the understanding of God and existence a long time, but then went against the natural flow of God, hence a world started. The world was not made in 7 days but was a result of the 7 understandings that produced an existence of what there is now. But to understand the real truth, you must truly give up your lift and give up all the world taught you, to enable you to become close then a part of your true creator. He wants to be understood and wants to give you all he has with amazing grace. He will fill your heart and keep the mind empty of the non-truth, and keep you full of understanding of the real truth. Be aware of what you truly are, then become the awareness then we can be as we truly are. God's companion of understanding.

JESUS

ALL EXISTENCES OF THE ELEMENTS OF UNDERSTANDING

| |

PASSED THROUGH THIS EXISTENCE BACK TO HIS FATHER OF UNDERSTANDIN

JESUS WAS HERE FOR THE GOOD OF GOD

THE UNDERSTANDING OF EXISTENCE SENT THE UNDERSTANDINGS SUN.

BIBLE

BECOME ONE APART OF THE ONENESS BUT LEFT OF THE EXISTENCE. READ THE BIBLE WITH THE LEFT OF YOUR MIND.
GOD'S WORLD = WARENESS OBEYED RECORDED RESPECTED, LOVED BY HIS DISCIPLES.

GOD'S WORLD = DISCIPLES WE ALL ARE TRULY WHEN WE LOVE AND RESPECT, WITH OBEDIENCE THE AWARENESS OF GOD.

ERM = EXISTENCE RECORDED RESPECT MASTER GOD.

NOW = NOTHING ONGOING FROM THE AWARENESS.
NOW = GOD'S TIME, NO PAST, NO PRESENT, NO FUTURE.

GOD

— THE EXISTENCES OF
— UNDERSTANDING SENT HIM DOWN TO SAVE THE WORLD

| |

— WILL PASS BACK DOWN THROUGH
— MAN WHO BECOMES AWARE OF THE UNDERSTANDING OF GOD AND OBEYS
SPREAD = SPEAK THE PHILOSOPHY OF THE RECORDINGS ABOUT THE EXISTENCE BY ALL DISCIPLES.
LOST = LACK OF OBEDIENCE SANCTIONED HIS TRUTH.

SAY = SPEAK ALL YOU KNOW.
SAVE = SANCTITY ALL VISITORS OF EXISTENCE.
HUMAN WORLD = WARENESS OBEYED RECORDED, LOST AND DAMNED.

HUMAN WORLD = AWARENESS OBEYED, RECORDED, LOST AND DAMNED.

ARE = AWARENESS RECORDED OF THE EXISTENCE OF GOD.
OH = OBEYANCE IN HONESTY OBEYING HONESTY.
AH = AWARENESS OF HONESTY.
A = AWARENESSLESS = UNAWARE OF THE AWARE.
OH NO = OBEYING THE HONESTY THAT YOU HAVE NOT OBEYED IN HONESTY.

THE AWARENESS WAS IN THE WORLD, AND OBEYED, RECORDED UNTO OTHERS, BUT THEN LOST BY THE DISCIPLES, HENCE GIVEN BACK TO GOD.

234

GONE = for god you have become a part of which you shall obey the respect of the nothingness of the existence of god.

END = The existences of nothing and understanding disciples of God. There is no end in the oneness.

SIN = no respect for the sanctuary given by God in the oneness of the nothingness.

NAME = In the nothingness or the awareness of the master's existence.

THINK = The truth, the honesty of one of the oneness of the nothingness and respect for the kindness given unto you by God.

| |

To those who are about to commit worldly acts.

TRINITY = You have found the truth and will give respect to the father of the oneness in the understanding that you are a part of one as a part of the oneness and will obey the nothingness as the truth to god

HOLY = In the honesty of the oneness with the love and respect of God to obey

MOTHER = Obedience to her master with the understanding of the oneness she shall obey the truth and honesty of her understanding of the existence and give respect to God, by the passing down of understanding unto her child of God.

LIE = Lack of understanding for the oneness and the existence.

SEE = Sanctuary in the existence of God by understanding the existence of nothingness.

HOUR = No one knows the hour until they know the hour. To be given the honesty and the obedience and understanding of Jesus Christ which you shall obey with respect.

JOY = One as a part of the oneness with the understanding of God and the obedience you give unto him for yonder.

PALM = In the protection awareness and love of my master.

PRAY = the Protection and respect of the awareness to ponder.

LIE = Lack of honesty to the oneness and the existence of God.

LIKE = The love for the oneness and respect for the kindness the existence gives you.

UN = Understanding of the nothingness.

THOU = The father of truth, honesty, obedience, love and understanding.

235

The thief that was a trial with Jesus, they kept the thief, because if they had sentenced the thief to death, hence they would have been sentencing themselves as they were him. But by keeping him they kept themselves and threw away their real self, which they were not ready for then. This is why Jesus asked his father to forgive them because he had only understanding for them. Humans at that time were not ready for the truth of Jesus Christ. Amen.

TODAY   =   YESTERDAY
              TOMORROW

<u>BEGINNING</u> = BEGINNING
   END

If you start at a beginning and go to what you call the end, the end is the centre of the beginning. So therefore there is no end to move a beginning from. A beginning is always the beginning until you invent an end.

If you cannot prove there was a beginning by proving there was a beginning then how can you prove the end when you have no beginning there to begin with? A beginning is a beginning and goes on beginning but never ending. There is no end.

There is no beginning because the end becomes the beginning therefore no end is either. What right do we have to invent a beginning when there is no end? You cannot prove an end, only a beginning because that's all there is.

All existences come from the existence of nothing. Any existence that moves away from the existence of the existence of the existence less self-moves back to the existence of where the existence came from, and leaves an existence of nothing. The beginning of all existences that begin, begin from nothing. All existences that go back to nothing begin being the existence of nothing. All existences that where the existence of nothing were existing as nothing therefore the nothingness was being an existence. All existences that come from nothing continue begging an existence of the nothingness that the existence was being before.

Existences come from being and go back to being nothing to being nothing – nothing.

THE EXISTENCE OF WHAT IS, IS BY THE EXISTENCE OF GOD, THAT, THAT IS NOT BY THE EXISTENCE OF GOD, AND HAS THE THINKING OF, IS NOT, THE EXISTENCE OF NOTHING, THAT IS, BY THE EXISTENCE OF GOD AND THAT THAT IS NOTHING, AND THOUGHT OF AS SOMETHING, IS NOT, THE EXISTENCE OF NOTHING, IS GOD, BUT THE EXISTENCE OF GOD AS SOMETHING, IS NOT, THE EXISTENCE OF THE EXISTENCE IS, BUT THE EXISTENCE OF SOMETHING, IS NOT.

THE NOTHING THAT MAKES THE EXISTENCE IS GOD, AND THE EXISTENCE OF GOD, IS THE NOTHINGNESS THAT IS PRODUCED, GOD CREATES THE NOTHINGNESS, WHICH PRODUCES THE EXISTENCE OF NOTHING, THE EXISTENCE OF NOTHING, IS THE EXISTENCE OF GOD, THE NOTHINGNESS CREATES THE NOTHING, THAT SHOES THE EXISTENCE OF GOD, GOD CREATES THE EXISTENCE OF NOTHING WHICH IS PRODUCED BY THE NOTHINGNESS, WHICH WAS MADE BY THE EXISTENCE OF GOD, THE EXISTENCE OF THE EXISTENCE, IS THE EXISTENCE OF NOTHING, AND THE NOTHINGNESS, IS THE CREATION OF GOD, GOD CREATES THE NOTHINGNESS, WHICH PRODUCES NOTHING, AND THE RESULT IS THE EXISTENCE OF NOTHING, WHICH IS THE EXISTENCE OF GOD.

ANY THING YOU ARE WANTING FROM THE WORLD AND FEEL THAT YOU NEED IS JUST HELPING IT TO CONTINUE IN THE WAY THAT IT IS SO IF YOU GIVE UP YOUR WORLDLY DESIRES THEN SOME PROGRESS CAN START IN A DIFFERENT WAY OF BEING.

YOU SEE YOU ARE NOT CONTENT WITH JUST YOURSELF TO BE CONTENT SO YOU HAVE TO GO OUT OR HAVE TO VIEW SOMETHING TO DO HENCE YOU KEEP IT ALL GOING ON.

YOU CAN NOT HAVE PEACE BY WANTING THE WORLD TO BE PEACEFUL. YOU MUST FIND IT WITHIN YOURSELF WHICH MEANS MAKING SACRIFICES FOR YOURSELF LIKE STOP THINKING THEN ONCE YOU FIND INNER PEACE THEN YOUR ACTIONS WILL CHANGE: NOTHING WILL GET TO YOU YOU WILL BE A PEACEFUL PERSON THEN BY YOUR ACTIONS OF PEACE OTHER PEOPLE WILL NOTICE AND TAKE THE SEED FROM YOU HENCE PEACE WILL BE PAST ON IN A TRULY PEACEFUL WAY BUT SO LONG AS YOU ARE PROTESTING ABOUT THIS AND ABOUT THAT THEN HOW CAN PEACE AND UNDERSTANDING BE SHOWN?

LET'S FACE IT, HOW WOULD YOU TRULY FEEL TO NEVER HAVE ANY MORE HANG-UPS OR PROBLEMS AGAIN. WELL YOU CAN DO THIS DO NOT LOOK FOR HAPPINESS FUN WHATEVER ANY MORE BECAUSE YOU KNOW IT CAN BE TAKEN AWAY AND THEN YOU HAVE FEELINGS OF SADNESS LOSS SO WHAT DO YOU DO? FIND PEACE AND CONTENTMENT WITHIN YOURSELF THEN YOU WILL BE IN THE MIDDLE WHICH IS NOTHING. DO NOT WANT FOR ANYTHING OTHER THAN WHAT YOU NEED AND KNOW THAT YOU NEED WHICH IS FOOD AND WATER HENCE NO FRUSTRATION. SO GIVE UP ONE THING THEN ANOTHER THEN ANOTHER KEEP MAKING THE FIRST STEPS FOR YOUR SELF THEN THE REST WILL FOLLOW.

DO REMEMBER IF YOU DO NOT GIVE UP YOUR WANTS FROM THE WORLD BECAUSE IT DOES THIS FOR YOU AND IF YOU DO NOT GIVE UP YOUR WANTING BECAUSE IT DOES NOT DO THAT FOR YOU THEN FOR YOU NO PEACE AND CONTENTMENT.......

AFTER ALL JUST LOOK AT YOUR SELF YOU ARE NO MORE THAN A CHILD IN A PLAYGROUND PLAYING GAMES AND NOT TRULY KNOWING OR LEARNING ANYTHING OTHER THAN TO PLAY GAMES. NOW GET RID OF ALL THAT THE WORLD HAS TAUGHT YOU AND START AGAIN, THIS TIME WITH TRUE UNDERSTANDING WHICH YOU WILL FIND WITHIN THE PEACE AND CONTENTMENT WITHIN YOU WHICH YOU HAVE BUT YOU MUST GIVE UP YOUR THINKING OF THE WORLD AND THINK OF IT NO MORE AND THEN BEGIN TO UNDERSTAND AND YOU WILL MAKE FALSE JUDGEMENTS NO MORE, JUST UNDERSTANDING.......

DO YOU FEEL THAT YOU HAVE HAD ENOUGH OF THE WORLD AND ALL THE PRESSURES YOU HAVE PICKED UP FROM IT.......

WELL LET ME TELL YOU SOMETHING NOW IS A CHANCE FOR YOU TO GIVE UP ALL YOUR WORLDLY THINGS THAT YOU THINK MAKE YOU HAPPY AND NOW FIND CONTENTMENT WITHIN YOURSELF.

LET ME START BY TELLING YOU THAT THE WORLD IS A STAGES, YES, AND LIKE A STAGE IT'S ALL MADE UP (NOT REAL, FALSE) THEREFORE ANYTHING THE WORLD GIVES YOU IS NOT REAL OR TRUE BECAUSE IT CAN BE TAKEN AWAY. SO ANYTHING YOU DO THAT YOU THINK MAKES YOU HAPPY WHAT HAPPENS WHEN THAT IS TAKEN AWAY? *WELL* YES THAT'S RIGHT, YOU BECOME UNHAPPY AND THEN YOUR MIND STARTS THINKING 'OH NO NOW WHAT AM I GOING TO DO?' SO YOUR MIND THINKS AND LOOKS FOR ANOTHER WORLDLY THING WHATEVER IT IS TO PUT YOU BACK IN HAPPINESS OR WHAT YOU THINK IS GOING TO MAKE YOU CONTENT.

NOW REMEMBER ANY OPINIONS OR JUDGEMENTS YOU HAVE ABOUT ANYTHING IS NOT TRUE. WHY FOR EXAMPLE IF YOU THINK THAT SOMEONE IS BAD OR UGLY THEN SOMETHING ELSE THINKS HE IS GOOD AND PRETTY THEN WHAT TRULY IS HE? WITHOUT YOUR OPINION OF WHAT YOU THINK GOOD BAD UGLY OR PRETTY IS WHAT TRULY IS HE?

THE PROBLEM WITH THE PEOPLE IN THE WORLD AND THE WORLD BEING THE WAY IT IS IS THAT YOU SAY THINGS ALL THE TIME AND DO THINGS ALL THE TIME AND YOU DO NOT KNOW WHAT YOU ARE DOING AND MOST OF WHAT YOU SAY IS NOT TRUE ALL YOU DO IS MAKE JUDGEMENTS TO SUIT YOURSELF AND CAN FIND NO ROOM FOR UNDERSTANDING WHAT A SHAME.

NOW GIVE IT ALL UP SO PEACE MAY BE GIVEN A REAL CHANCE TO PREVAIL BECAUSE AFTER ALL IF YOU DO NOT FIND REAL PEACE WITHIN YOURSELF AND MAKE THE FIRST STEP THEN HOW CAN OTHERS PICK UP THE SEED. SO YOU MAKE THE SACRIFICE GIVE UP YOUR TINY DECEITFUL WORLD AND FIND THE TRUTH THEN THE NEXT PERSON CAN PICK SOMETHING SOLID UP FROM YOU INSTEAD OF THE WORLD'S NONSENSE THAT YOU HAVE BEEN CONSTANTLY PASSING ON.

AND ALL YOU HAVE TO DO IS STOP THINKING, YES, STOP THINKING

GIVE YOUR MIND A CHANCE TO WORK AS IT REALLY SHOULD

THEN PEACE AND CONTENTMENT SHALL BEGIN ITS COURSE FOR YOU.......

THE EXISTENCE OF NOTHING EXISTS WHEN YOU SEE AN EXISTENCE, AN EXISTENCE ONLY EXISTS AS AN EXISTENCE IS BEING SEEN BEFORE YOU SAW THE EXISTENCE, BUT IF NOT FOR ANYONE SEEING AN EXISTENCE THEN THE EXISTENCE IS EXISTENCELESS TO US, AN EXISTENCE IS EXISTANTLESS BEFORE WE SEE THE EXISTENCE, AN EXISTENCE EXISTS BECAUSE YOU CAN SEE THE EXISTENCE, THEREFORE WE CAN SEE THE EXISTENCE EXISTS IF SEEN, THEN AFTER THE EXISTENCE HAS BEEN SEEN THEN YOU HAVE AN EXISTENCE, BUT BEFORE THAT OF THE EXISTENCE, THEN THE EXISTENCE IS EXISTANTLESS, WHAT YOU CAN NOT SEE WHICH HAS NOT BEEN SEEN IS EXISTENTLESS TO YOU, THE EXISTENCE OF AN EXISTENCE IS NOTHING, BUT THE EXISTENTLESS IS NOTHING AT ALL HENCE NOTHINGNESS, THE EXISTENTLESS DOES NOT EXIST AS AN EXISTENCE, THE EXISTENTLESS GOES BEYOND THE NOTHINGNESS, BECAUSE THE EXISTENCE DOES NOT EXIST AT ALL BEFORE THE EXISTENTLESS HAS BEEN SEEN BY ANY MAN, BUT WHEN YOU SEE THE EXISTENTLESS, THEN AN EXISTENCE COMES FROM THE EXISTENTLESS AND EXISTS AS A NOTHING AND AS A PART OF THE NOTHINGNESS.

THE EXISTENCE OF NOTHING EXISTS, WHEN YOU SEE WHAT EXISTS, AND IS AN EXISTENCE BEFORE YOU OR ANY MAN SAW THE EXISTENCE, BECAUSE WHAT MAN HAS NOT SEEN AND NEVER SEEN TO HIM THE EXISTENCE IS EXISTENTLESS, BUT YOUR EXISTENTLESS HAS ALL READY BEEN SEEN BY GOD, SO THE EXISTENTLESS HAS ALWAYS BEEN AN EXISTENCE AND EXISTS IN THE EYE OF GOD, SO THE EXISTENTLESS ONLY EXISTS WITH MAN, BUT IN FACT THE EXISTENTLESS DOES NOT EXISTS AT ALL BECAUSE THE EXISTENTLESS EXISTS AS A PART OF THE EXISTENCE OF GOD.

NOW IS THE TIME FOR US ALL TO COME TOGETHER AS TRULY ONE, THIS INVOLVES US ALL COMING TO THE UNDERSTANDING OF OURSELVES AND EACH OTHER AND GOD.

WE ARE ALL ONE IN FLESH AND BLOOD BUT BECAUSE WE THINK, THIS IS WHAT SPLITS THE ONENESS; HENCE YOU HAVE A WORLD AS IT IS TODAY. ONCE YOU CAN UNDERSTAND WHAT IS REAL AND WHAT IS NOT, THE PROGRESS IS BEGINNING. THE SUN THE MOON AND UNIVERSE ARE REAL, BUT ONLY EXIST AS AN EXISTENCE OF NOTHING, BUT YOU DO NOT AT THE MOMENT UNDERSTAND THAT. BY CALLING IT THE MOON OR THE SUN, WE ARE PUTTING UNREALISM ON REALISM, THEREFORE YOU SEE THE EXISTENCE NOT AS THE EXISTENCE TRULY IS, BUT AS THE NAME WE HAVE PUT THERE.

THE ONLY WAY TO SEE REALISM AS THE EXISTENCE TRULY IS, IS TO BE THOUGHTLESS OF THE NAME AND BE IN CLEAR MINDEDNESS, THEN ONCE YOU CAN SEE NOT AS WE CALL THE EXISTENCE BUT HOW THE EXISTENCE TRULY EXIST AS THE EXISTENCE TRULY IS. THEN YOU WILL UNDERSTAND THAT EVERYTHING WE HAVE MADE, AND IS NOT MADE BY THE NATURAL ELEMENTS OF GOD IS NOT REAL AT ALL, BUT IT EXISTS IN THE UNREAL WORLD. TO LOSE THE PERCEPTION OF HOW MAN THE HUMAN SEE THINGS, WHICH IS UNREAL IS TRULY BLISS, AND TO SEE EXISTENCES AS THEY TRULY EXIST FILLS YOU WITH UNDERSTANDING AND KNOWING OF REALISM AND GOD. SO UNDERSTAND WHAT YOU SEE THAT IS COMPILED BY HUMANS IS THE EXISTENCE OF NOTHING IN THE UNREAL SENSE, AND WHAT YOU SEE THAT HAS NOT BEEN COMPILED BY MAN IS THE EXISTENCE OF NOTHING IN THE REAL SENSE. HENCE YOU WILL HAVE NO REGARD FOR HUMAN THINGS, AND HAVE MUCH REGARD FOR THAT WHICH TRULY EXISTS AS NOTHING WHICH IS A PART OF GOD.

WHEN YOU GIVE SOMETHING, WHEN YOU HAVE UNDERSTANDING OF THE NOTHINGNESS, THEN YOU WILL GIVE FROM YOUR CHARITY WITHOUT EVER EXPECTING BACK. BECAUSE YOU UNDERSTAND THE UNREALISM OF THINGS, AND THAT WHEN YOU GIVE A THING, YOU ARE AXIALLY NOT GIVING ANYTHING AT ALL TO THEM THAT THEY WILL TRULY HAVE, HENCE YOU WILL WANT NOTHING IN RETURN BECAUSE YOU UNDERSTAND YOURSELF, AND GIVE WHAT YOU HAVE BECAUSE YOU UNDERSTAND OTHERS. ALSO YOUR CHARITY OF GIVING WILL BE YOUR UNDERSTANDING OF OTHERS AS THEY ARE, AND KNOWING THAT IF THEY TAKE A SEED, YOU HAVE TRULY GIVEN THEM SOMETHING OF WHICH THEY WILL TRULY KEEP, AND KNOW THAT IF THEY TAKE IT, AND UNDERSTAND IT, THEN IN RETURN THEY HAVE GIVEN YOU UNDERSTANDING, BUT IF THEY DO NOT TAKE IT THEN YOU WILL HAVE THE UNDERSTANDING OF THAT.

WHEN YOU HAVE FAITH THEN YOU DO WHAT YOU DO FROM THE UNDERSTANDING OF THE FAITH, HENCE YOU ARE ABLE TO PASS IT ONTO OTHERS THROUGH YOUR ACTIONS OF UNDERSTANDING. WHATEVER SITUATION YOU ARE IN, WITH YOUR UNDERSTANDING YOU WILL BE ABLE TO DO BY YOUR FAITH OF WHICH YOU UNDERSTAND. YOUR FAITH AND UNDERSTANDING WILL BE YOUR GRACEFULNESS WHICH COMES FROM YOUR FAITH, THEN WHEN PEOPLE WANT TO UNDERSTAND YOU HAVE THE FAITH TO SPEAK ONLY THE TRUTH.

WHEN YOU HAVE HOPE THEN YOU HOPE ONLY THAT ALL WILL KNOW GOD, AND THAT THOSE WHO DO NOT KNOW GOD AND YOU KNOW IT THROUGH THEIR ACTIONS OF THE WORLD, THEN YOU WILL NOT JUDGE THEM OR HOLD WITH YOU A BETTER TONGUE, BUT JUST HOPE THEY WILL KNOW GOD BECAUSE YOU UNDERSTAND WHAT GOD REQUIRES AND WITH YOUR FAITH YOU SHALL GIVE IT.

WHILST YOU ARE IN THE WORLD START UNDERSTANDING
YOURSELF SO YOU MAY THEN HAVE UNDERSTANDING OF
THE WORLD TO BE UNDERSTANDING THE TRUTH WHICH
IS TO UNDERSTAND GOD THEN TO BE PASSING ON THE
UNDERSTANDING SO THAT THE NEXT GENERATION CAN
BE GROWING UP WITH THE UNDERSTANDING SO THEY
MAY EXIST BY THE UNDERSTANDING SO THERE MAY BE
GRACEFUL PEACE AND CONTENTMENT ON EARTH BEING
A PART OF GOD'S WORLD.

HAVE LOVE SO YOU MAY GIVE IT
HAVE FAITH SO YOU MAY SHARE IT
HAVE CHARITY SO YOU MAY BE CHARITABLE
HAVE HOPE SO YOU MAY HOPE ALL WILL KNOW GOD
HAVE CONTENTMENT SO YOU MAY BE CONTENT
HAVE GRACE SO YOU MAY BE GRACEFUL
HAVE SELFLESSNESS SO YOU MAY BE SELFLESS
HAVE RESPECT SO YOU MAY GIVE IT
HAVE INNER STRENGTH SO YOU MAY KEEP IT
FOR GOD.

YOU HAVE THE MIND
TO TAKE THE KNOWLEDGE
TO HAVE THE THOUGHT
OF THE WORD UNDERSTAND
TO KNOW
THE TRUTH
OF GOD
WHICH IS THE EXISTENCE
OF

IF MAN TRULY KNEW GOD THEN WE WOULD KNOW NOTHING GOD WOULD BE ABLE TO DO HIS WORK AND ALL WE WOULD KNOW WOULD BE THE EXISTENCE.

SO LONG AS THERE IS A WORLD WHERE PEOPLE THINK THEY KNOW THEN GOD CANNOT PREVAIL HENCE NO PEACE AND CONTENTMENT ON EARTH.

BECAUSE PEOPLE ONLY KNOW WHAT THEY HAVE BEEN TOLD BY OTHERS MEANS THAT THEY HAVE TO COME TO THEIR OWN TRUTH BECAUSE THAT'S ALL THEY HAVE. NOW IF YOU GIVE UNTO THEM A BIT OF THE REAL TRUTH BECAUSE IT IS SO FAR AWAY FROM THE WORLD'S TRUTH THEY OFTEN GET FRIGHTENED AND DEFENSIVE.

PEOPLE ARE OFTEN FRIGHTENED OF WHAT THEY CANNOT UNDERSTAND SO UNDERSTAND THEM.

IF YOU TRULY BECOME A PART OF GOD THEN YOU WILL BE OUT OF THE WORLD AND IN THE TRUTH BUT THEN YOU MUST TREAT THE WORLD YOU LEFT BEHIND WITH UNDERSTANDING AND GRACE BECAUSE THIS IS WHAT GOD DEMANDS.

REMEMBER PEOPLE IN THE WORLD DO NOT KNOW WHAT THEY ARE DOING SO DO NOT JUDGE THEM OR HOLD WITH YOU A BITTER TONGUE BECAUSE AS SOON AS YOU DO THIS YOU WILL HAVE TO BE THINKING AND AS SOON AS YOU DO THAT YOU WILL BE PULLED BACK IN THE WORLD

AND LOSE YOU UNDERSTANDING AND WILL NO LONGER BE WITH GOD.

REMEMBER: GOD REQUIRES YOUR WORLD
REQUIRES YOU PAST
REQUIRES YOU'RE THINKING MIND
SO THEN YOU HAVE NO WORLD NO
PAST NO THINKING

REWARD: NO WEIGHT OF THE WORLD AS EMPTY
MIND OF THINKING
A WARM HEART UNDERSTANDING
THOUGHTS OF UNDERSTANDING
THE TRUTH A PART OF GOD'S WORLD.

IF YOU DO THIS THEN YOU WILL HAVE SOLIDNESS INSIDE YOU AND NO LONGER REQUIRE WHAT THE HUMAN WORLD HAS TO OFFER.

BE A PART OF IT WITHOUT BEING A PART OF IT THEN YOU WILL HAVE NOTHING TO DO WITH IT AND PEACE MAY PREVAIL.

THE CORRUPTION OF TELEVISION, RADIO, AND NEWSPAPERS IS THAT IT ALL TAKES YOU AWAY FROM THE REAL TRUTH AND TAKES YOU AWAY FROM YOUR REAL SELF. IT INVADES ON YOU A LOAD OF UNREALISMS, NO TRUTH. THE FACT IS THAT YOU'RE INFLUENCED BY IT, IF YOU READ A NEWSPAPER THEN IT IS INFLUENCING YOU TO BE KNOWLEDGEABLE OF THE WORLD, HENCE YOU SPREAD IT IN CONVERSATION AND YOU THINK YOU KNOW SOMETHING.

ALSO THE PAPERS AND TV ARE CAPABLE IN INFLUENCING PEOPLE INTO DOING WHAT HAS BEND ONE PLUS TAKES YOU UP AND DOWN IN EMOTIONS IN ITS UNREALISM.

WHEN ALL MEDIA HAS GONE FOR GOOD, THEN PEOPLE CAN EMPTY THEIR MINDS AND FIND GOD WITHIN THEM. BUT AT THE MOMENT ALL YOU'RE GETTING IS THE WORLD'S DOINGS WHICH REALLY HAS NOTHING TO DO WITH YOU AT ALL, THE CHILDREN SHOULD NEVER SEE TV OR PAPERS OR HEAR OF THE WORLD'S EVENTS, IT IS AN INVASION ON THEIR INNOCENCE AND TAKES THEM AWAY FROM WHAT THEY SHOULD BE TRULY UNDERSTANDING AND KNOWING, HENCE IT CORRUPTS YOUNG MINDS. THE YOUNG MIND SHOULD BE KEPT FREE OF WORLDLY THOUGHTS, THEN WHEN THEY GROW UP WITH CLEAR MINDS THEN THEIR WORLD WILL BE NONE OF WHAT GOES ON TODAY, HENCE THEIR CHILDREN WILL LEARN THE TRUE WAY OF BEING AND EXISTING AND BE ABLE TO HAVE REAL UNDERSTANDING, INSTEAD OF THE UNREAL UNDERSTANDING OF THE WORLD. THE WORLD AS IT IS TODAY HAS TO GET RID OF ALL IT HAS MADE FOR ITSELF, TO BECOME IT'S REAL SELF IN THE REAL WORLD OF GOD.

THE ONLY TRUE PERSPECTIVE THERE IS FOR MAN TO HAVE, IS THE PERFECTION OF UNDERSTANDING AND KNOWING.

ANYTHING IN THE WORLD THAT MAN TRIES TO FIND FOR HIS PERFECTION DOES NOT EXIST, AND IF HE THINKS HE HAS GOT IT THEN IT IS UNREAL. SO FIND UNDERSTANDING FOR YOURSELF WITHIN YOU THEN YOU WILL HAVE PERFECTION FO UNDERSTANDING, WHICH IS A BLESSING OF GOD, BUT YOU MUST COME OUT OF THE WORLD BOTH IN SPIRIT AND IN MIND.

START FINDING PEACE IN YOUR SELF NOW SO OTHERS CAN PICK UP PEACE. IF YOU FIND PEACE AND CONTENTMENT WITHIN THEN YOU WILL CHANGE AND THE NEXT PERSON CAN NOTICE IT AND SAY 'WHAT HAVE YOU GOT THAT THEY HAVE NOT?' AND THIS WILL BE PEACE WITHIN BECAUSE UNLESS YOU START TO CHANGE THEN THERE WILL BE NO CHANGE FOR THE GOOD OF MAN AND THINGS WILL JUST GO ON IN THE FASHION THAT THEY HAVE BEEN AND YOU MUST ADMIT IT'S NOT GOD FOR YOU, IS IT? NO. WELL THEN CHANGE FIND UNDERSTANDING FOR OTHERS INSTEAD OF MAKING JUDGEMENTS ABOUT PEOPLE AND THINGS AND GIVE UP YOUR OPINIONS SO THE NEXT PERSON CAN LEARN A DIFFERENT WAY OF BEING OTHER THAN WHAT THE WORLD HAS TAUGHT THEM. AT THE MOMENT EVERYTHING IS IN CHAOS YOU LOSE YOUR TEMPER YOU ARE IMPATIENT. BASICALLY YOU ARE HUMAN AND SO LONG AS YOU CONTINUE TO BE HUMAN THEN EVERYONE ELSE WILL CONTINUE HENCE NO PEACE FOR YOU SO FIND YOUR INNER PEACE SO YOU MAY PLANT THE SEED FOR THE NEXT PERSON AND THEN PEOPLE WILL BEGIN TO BE MORE CONTENT WITH THEMSELVES AND STOP SEEKING WHAT THE WORLD HAS TO OFFER WHICH IS BASICALLY CONFUSION AND CHAOS. IT IS UP TO YOU TO MAKE THE REAL CHANGE BY FIRST MAKING THE CHANGE IN YOU WITHIN YOU THEN IT CAN SPREAD AND WHO KNOWS BUT GOD MAYBE UTOPIA BUT YOU HAVE GOT TO BE WILLING TO MAKE THE SACRIFICE FOR YOURSELF SO YOU MAY BE CONTENTFUL AND PEACEFUL THEN OTHERS CAN EE AND LEARN BY YOU BUT YOU MUST MAKE THE FIRST STEPS THEN THE REST WILL COME.

TO KNOW SOMETHING AND KNOW THAT YOU KNOW IS SOMETHING YOU WILL NEVER HAVE UNLESS YOU STOP THINKING ABOUT COME OUT FROM THE WORLD WHICH YOU HAVE BEEN A PART OF AND LET'S FACE IT,

WHAT HAVE YOU REALLY GOT SO IT CAN NEVER BE TAKEN AWAY BY ANYBODY. WELL EXACTLY, YOU HAVE NOTHING, FIND SOMETHING WITHIN YOUR TRUE SELF (WHICH HAS NO SELF AT ALL) AND THAT WILL NEVER BE ABLE TO BE TAKEN AWAY AND WHAT IS THAT YOU TRULY HAVE WITHIN YOURSELF IT IS TRUE LOVE, TRUE UNDERSTANDING, TRUE PEACE AND CONTENTMENT AND A WARM HEART BUT TO GET THIS WHICH ONCE YOU HAVE YOU ARE IN PARADISE AND IT CANNOT BE TAKEN AWAY YOU MUST GIVE UP ALL THAT THE WORLD TAUGHT YOU AND ALL YOU TOOK FROM IT.

I KNOW THAT YOU HAVE THAT STRONG FEELING TO LIVE A LIFE AND BE PART OF IT THAT'S ONLY BECAUSE YOU ARE SCARED OF MISSING OUT LOSING SOMETHING THAT YOU HAVE NOT TRULY GOT BUT UNDERSTAND AND TRULY UNDERSTAND THAT IT IS ALL NOTHING THEN YOU WILL TRULY KNOW AND KNOW THAT YOU KNOW THAT THE WORLD IS NOT WORTH PLAYING WITH ANYMORE HENCE YOU MAY FIND PEACE WITHIN.

ALL THE WORLD HAS GIVEN YOU IS HOW TO PLAY THE PART IT TAKES YOU UP IN HAPPINESS ONE MINUTE AND DOWN IN UNHAPPINESS THE NEXT SO ALL THE TIME YOU ARE GOING UP AND DOWN, UP AND DOWN, GOING NOWHERE LEARNING NOTHING UNDERSTANDING NOTHING, HENCE CONFUSION NOW UNDERSTAND THE TRUE NOTHINGNESS OF THE WORLD AND ALL OF IT THEN YOU CAN FIND PLENTY OF TIME FINDING YOUR TRUE SELF WHICH HAS NOTHING TO DO WITH THE WORLD THAT HUMANS HAVE INVENTED FOR HIS OWN PLAYGROUND.

SO JUST DO WHAT YOU HAVE TO DO TO BE HERE ON EARTH WHICH IS EAT AND RINK THAT IS ALL YOU TRULY HAVE TO DO AND REPRODUCE ANYTHING ELSE THAT YOU THINK YOU HAVE TO DO WITHOUT TRULY KNOWING MEANS YOU DO NOT HAVE TO DO IT AT ALL SO GIVE IT UP THEN PEACE MAY PREVAIL.......

LISTEN AND LISTEN CAREFULLY ALL YOU HAVE TO DO IS STOP THINKING, IT IS A PHYSICAL EXERCISE, TAKE DEEP BREATHS, SQUINT YOUR EYES, YOU WILL FIND A WAY TO BLOCK OUT YOUR THINKING. THEN AFTER A WHILE WHEN YOU COME TO REALISE THAT YOUR THINKING OF WORRY, ANGER, JEALOUSY IS ALL IN THE MIND AND CAN BE GOT RID OF BY NOT THINKING, THEN YOU WILL BEGIN NOT RELATING TO THEM BECAUSE YOU WILL UNDERSTAND THAT THEY DO NOT EXIST UNLESS YOU HOLD ONTO THEM. HENCE YOUR OWN THOUGHTS THAT YOU WERE THINKING WILL MEAN NOTHING TO YOU, THEN WHAT THE WORLD TAUGHT YOU WILL GO AND YOU WILL LEARN THE OTHER WAY OF BEING AND PEACE WILL SET IN.

AFTER THAT PROGRESS WHATEVER COMES INTO YOUR MIND, EXAMPLE SUBCONSCIOUS THOUGHTS MAYBE OF DESIRE YOU HAVE ALWAYS HAD FOR SOMETHING, OR WHEN YOU REMEMBER SOMETHING FROM THE PAST THAT HAS ALWAYS UPSET YOU, FROM THE TIME IT HAPPENED AND TO THE TIME YOU THINK ABOUT IT BECAUSE YOU WERE UNABLE TO UNDERSTAND IT AT THE TIME. NOW YOU HAVE A MIND FREE FROM THE WORLD MEANS THAT YOU WILL BE ABLE TO UNDERSTAND ALL YOUR SUBCONSCIOUS INSTEAD OF ASKING WHY THIS OR WHY THAT OR HOLDING RESENTMENTS, HENCE YOU WILL HAVE NO FEELING ABOUT THEM BECAUSE THEY HAVE BEEN UNDERSTOOD, WHICH WAS WHAT THEY WERE LOOKING FOR IN THE FIRST PLACE. ALAS THEY WILL MEAN NOTHING TO YOU ANY MORE. THEY WILL GO YOU WILL BE FREE.

YOU MUST KEEP WORKING ALL THE TIME KEEPING THE WORLDLY THOUGHTS AT BAY, AND UNDERSTANDING ANY SUBCONSCIOUS THOUGHTS, HENCE KEEPING A CLEAR MIND, PEACE AND CONTENTMENT WITHIN YOU.

UNDERSTANDING IN THE END IS ALL YOU WILL BE LEFT WITH, YOU WILL NOT JUDGE ANYONE AS GOOD OF BAD

BECAUSE YOU WILL UNDERSTAND THEM. YOU WILL BECOME GRACEFUL IN YOUR UNDERSTANDING, AND YOU WILL NOT HAVE THE NEED TO DO MANY OF THE THINGS IN THE WORLD THAT YOU DO BECAUSE YOU WILL UNDERSTAND THE NOTHINGNESS OF IT ALL. IF YOU DO NOT THINK OF ANYTHING AS YOU THINK IT IS, THEN THE TRUTH IS, THAT IT'S SOMETHING THAT IS WHY THERE IS NO TRUTH IN THE WORLD, BECAUSE EVERYTHING IS ONLY WHAT PEOPLE THINK IT IS, BUT IF YOU DO NOT THINK THEN YOU WILL UNDERSTAND TRULY THAT IS NOTHING.

UNLOAD ALL THAT THE WORLD HAS TAUGHT YOU AND STEP INTO THE REAL SIDE OF EXISTENCE. THERE IS ONLY PEACE AND LOVE OF UNDERSTANDING, CONTENTMENT, GRACE, TRUE KNOWING, AND GOD.

ALL WONDERS OF THE UNIVERSE WILL BE OPENED UP TO YOU THROUGH THE NOTHINGNESS, IF YOU JUST LET YOUR MAD UP SELF THAT THE WORLD HAS GIVEN YOU AND BECOME YOUR REAL SELF WHICH HAS NO SELF THEN YOU WILL BE A PART OF THE UNDERSTANDING WHICH YOU ARE, INSTEAD OF THE GAME MAN HAS PLAYED FOR HIS OWN EGO, WHICH HE HAS DESERVED HIMSELF WITH FOR SO LONG.

IT IS CALLED IN RELATIVES TERMS NOT BEING HUMAN, AND BEING TRULY WHAT YOU ARE WHICH IS A PART OF THE UNIVERSE AND THE UNDERSTANDING WHICH MAKES IT.

TO TRULY KNOW GOD, IS TO TRULY KNOW YOURSELF YOUR REAL SELF, NOT THE SELF THAT YOU HAVE BEEN GIVEN BY THE WORLD, (WHICH IS NOT OUR REAL SELF) BUT YOUR TRUE SELF WHICH IS IN THE UNDERSTANDING OF JESUS CHRIST, WHO WAS SELFLESS. WHAT YOU ARE NOW IS AN IMAGE OF WHAT MAN THINKS HE SHOULD BE, RATHER THAN KNOWING WHAT WE TRULY WOULD BE IF WE ALL KNEW GOD, THE WHEN THE DAY COMES THAT YOU TRULY KNOW GOD THEN YOU WILL BE AS HE TRULY KNOWS YOU TO BE, INSTEAD OF WHAT MAN THINKS HE IS. YOU ARE MADE UP OF MANY DIFFERENT CHARACTERS AND YOU USE THEM ALL IN DIFFERENT SITUATIONS, HENCE YOU PLAY THE GAME OF LIFE. NOW YOU'RE TRUE SELF IS EMPTY OF ALL THESE PEOPLE THAT HAVE BEEN PUT INSIDE OF YOU SO FOR NOW YOU ARE STUCK WITH THEM. STOP THINKING AS THE WORLD HAS TAUGHT YOU AND YOU MAY BEGIN TO FIND YOUR REAL SELF AND THROUGH UNDERSTANDING ALL WORLDLY WAYS THAT HAVE BEEN DUMPED THERE IN YOU WILL GO AND WHAT A RELIEF.

SO YOU GO THROUGH HUMAN EMOTIONS BECAUSE YOU HAVE SEEN THEM, THEY HAVE BEEN GIVEN TO YOU, AND YOU HAVE TAKEN THEM. SO ALL THE TIME YOU ARE BEING GIVEN TO BY THE WORLD AND TAKING IT ONE MOMENT, THEN IT TAKES IT BACK THE NEXT, SO ANYTHING YOU ARE GIVEN OR ARE TAKING FROM THE WORLD IS NOT TRUE BECAUSE IT DOES NOT LAST OR MEANS ANYTHING TO YOU OF ANY REAL VALUE AND ALL YOU ARE LEFT WITH IS AN EXTRA BUILD UP OF WORLDLY RUBBISH INSIDE YOU WHICH YOU DID NOT TRULY NEED IN THE BEGINNING. AND IT HELPS TO MAKE YOU SOMETHING THAT YOU ARE NOT AND DO NOT DESERVE.

FIND THE TRUE UNDERSTANDING OF THE NOTHINGNESS OF THE WORLD, THEN UNDERSTAND IT THEN YOU WILL FIND GOD AND HE WILL GIVE YOU THE REST,

HENCE YOU WILL NEED THE UNREAL OFFERINGS OF THE WORLD NO MORE. PULLS YOU WILL BE CLEAN OF ALL THE BUILD UP OF ALL YOUR FALSENESS AND CLEAN OF THE WORLD PIT.

TO BE EMPTY INSIDE OF THE HUMAN WAY IS BLISS AND PARADISE, THEN WHEN YOU REACH THIS FAR YOU WILL UNDERSTAND AND HAVE TRUE LOVE AND THAT'S ALL YOU WILL GIVE TO ANYBODY AND EVERYBODY, AND THIS IS THE ONLY WAY TO HAVE PEACE AND CONTENTMENT ON EARTH. SO FIRST FIND YOUR INNER PEACE, SO YOU ARE TRULY AT PEACE, THEN OTHERS CAN FOLLOW SUIT.

TO KNOW GOD IS TO KNOW NOTHING HENCE FREEDOM FROM THE WORLD AND ITS CHAOS.......

TO TRULY KNOW NOTHING, IS TO KNOW GOD, FOR THEN THE FLOW OF THE UNIVERSE WILL GUIDE YOU THROUGH SAFELY. GOD WILL ALWAYS BE THERE TO GIVE YOU UNDERSTANDING AND WITH JESUS YOU MAY WALK. YOU ARE NOT HERE FOR ANY PURPOSE THAT MAN TELLS YOU YOU ARE HERE FOR OR FOR ANY THAT YOU THINK YOU ARE HERE FOR.

THE TRUTH IS YOU ARE HERE EXISTING TO BE A PART OF THE HUGE SURROUNDINGS THAT SURROUND US, AND TO KNOW THE EXISTENCE OF NOTHING AND UNDERSTAND GOD.

SO AS SOON AS YOU CAN STOP FEEDING THE WORLD AND CONTINUING TO BE A PART OF THE PLAYGROUND, THEN YOU CAN GROW UP IN THE TRUE SENSE OF THE WORD, THEN OTHERS CAN FOLLOW, BUT CONTINUE TO PLAY THE PART THEN YOU WILL ALWAYS DO AS A CHILD IN THE WORLD WOULD DO PLAYING GAMES. AND WHERE DOES IT LEAD YOU OR WHAT DOES IT REALLY GIVE AND DO FOR YOU, WHEN EVERYBODY STEPS DOWN FROM THE WORLD, THEN THERE WILL BE NO MORE PAIN OR NO MORE FALSENESS TO COVER IT UP WITH. THEN WE ARE LEFT WITH GOD-NOTHING-EXISTENCE INSTEAD OF LIES-SOMETHING-LIVING.

DO IT FOR YOURSELF, DO IT FOR THE WORLD SO THE BABIES BEING BORN WILL BE BORN IN GOD'S WORLD OF NO SUFFERING INSTEAD OF THE WORLD OF HUMAN EMOTION.

WHEN UTOPIA COMES WHEN WE ALL FIND GOD THEN WE WILL SEE THE END

OF HOW IT SHOULD NOT HAVE BEEN
AND EXIST TO OUR END OF HOW IT SHOULD BE.

EVERYBODY IS A PART OF GOD, AND WE ARE ALL ONE (A PART OF THE ONENESS) BUT WE THINK THEREFORE THAT IS WHAT MAKES US DIFFERENT, AND DISTANT FROM GOD.

NOW GIVE UP YOUR THINKING THEN YOU WILL UNDERSTAND JESUS, BUT YOU HAVE TO GIVE UP YOUR WORLD, TO BE ABLE TO RECEIVE REALNESS RATHER THAN THE UNREALNESS THAT YOU AVE AT THE MOMENT.

WHEN YOU SAY, "OH IT'S NOTHING" YOU DO NOT REALISE HOW TRUE THAT IS, SO START TO UNDERSTAND IT BY ITS TRUE MEANING AND SHOULD BE UNDERSTOOD FOR YOU TO BE ABLE TO KNOW WHAT PEACE IS, WHAT CONTENTMENT IS, WHAT GOD IS. THE TRUTH IS NOTHING THAT'S THE TRUTHLESS TRUTH, THE EXISTENCE OF NOTHING IS THE EXISTENCE OF GOD, AND THROUGH THESE UNDERSTANDINGS COMES WHAT JESUS HAD. JESUS HAD EVERYTHING THAT WE TRULY HAVE WITHIN US NOW YOU GET IT, GIVE UP YOUR LIFE FOR GOD, THE TRUTH, THEN PEACE ON EARTH SHALL PREVAIL INSTEAD OF MAN'S WAY OF THINKING.

BECAUSE THERE IS NO PAST OR PRESENT OR FUTURE UNLESS YOU THINK ABOUT, THAT'S WHY GOD REQUIRES IT BECAUSE IT IS NOT REAL AND HE WILL RELIEVE YOU OF WHAT THE HUMAN WORLD HAS INVENTED FOR YOU, BECAUSE GOD WILL GIVE UNTO YOU ONLY THE TRUTH, WHICH REQUIRES FROM YOU NO PAST PRESENT OR FUTURE. HENCE GOD WANTS TO SAVE YOU FROM THINKING OF THE HUMAN UNREALISM, AND YOU WILL BE SAVED AND REBORN AS YOU WAS BORN KNOWING NOTHING.

HOW MANY TIMES DO YOU SAY TO YOURSELF "I WISH I COULD HAVE PEACE OF MIND" WHY DO YOU SAY THAT, BECAUSE IN PEACE OF MIND THERE IS NOTHING TO TOUCH YOU AND THE WORLD CAN NOT GET TO YOU,

BUT YOU MUST WORK ON KEEPING IT OUT, HENCE NOT RELATING TO WORLDLY THOUGHTS SO THEY WILL HAVE NO GROUNDS ON WHICH TO STAY. AFTER A WHILE YOU WILL BE ABLE TO UNDERSTAND WORLDLY THOUGHTS WHICH WANT TO PULL YOU BACK INTO THE WORLD, AND THOUGHTS OF UNDERSTANDING WHICH WILL GIVE YOU UNDERSTANDING FOR YOUR INNER PEACE, HENCE STAYING WITH THE TRUTH AND GOD.

HOW DO YOU THINK JESUS WAS ABLE TO HAVE SUCH UNDERSTANDING, SUCH FAITH AND GRACE, WELL IT WAS NOT BY THINKING ABOUT IT THAT'S FOR SURE IT WAS POSSIBLE FOR HIM TO DO AND SAY WHAT HE DID THROUGH NOT THINKING, BUT BY UNDERSTANDING AND HAVING THE THOUGHT OF UNDERSTANDING SO HE COULD PUT INTO WORDS FOR US TO TAKE HIS UNDERSTANDING AND UNDERSTAND. NOBODY ON THIS PLANET (NO HUMAN THAT IS) CAN DO ANYONE THING FOR A, IN RELATIVE TERMS, LONG TIME BY THINKING ABOUT IT, WHY BECAUSE AFTER A WHILE THE MIND GETS TIRED, BUT IF YOU DO NOT THINK BUT JUST HAVE THOUGHTS ON UNDERSTANDING HENCE NO BOREDOM NO TIREDNESS NO STRESS NO ANYTHING THAT IS A PRODUCTION OF THE HUMAN BEING. YOU WILL ONLY BE AT PEACE WITH YOURSELF.

NOW BECAUSE JESUS UNDERSTOOD THE NOTHINGNESS OF THE WORLD (THE HUMAN THINKING WORLD) HENCE HE HAD THE FAITH AND UNDERSTANDING TO STAY OUT OF IT, BECAUSE HE UNDERSTOOD IT, BECAUSE HE KNEW GOD.

WHEN JESUS WENT INTO THE MARKET PLACE WHERE THE PEOPLE SAY HE LOST HIS TEMPER, HE DID NOT LOSE HIS TEMPER BUT MERELY DEMONSTRATED WHAT WOULD BE AS A RESULT OF BUYING AND SELLING USING MONEY, AND YES HE SHOWED THE RESULT AND PEOPLE DO WHAT HE DID THEN, BUT THEY LOSE THEIR TEMPER AND GET ANGRY AND ALL THAT, NOW WHEN THEY SAW HIM DOING WHAT HE WAS DOING IN THE MARKET THEY SHOULD HAVE COME TO THE UNDERSTANDING THAT YES THIS IS HOW WE WILL BEHAVE AND WE WILL CAUSE DAMAGE TO OURSELVES UNLESS WE COME TO SENSES, AND THAT'S WHY JESUS DID WHAT HE DID, BUT THIS DID NOT WORK, IT DID NOT HAPPEN, BECAUSE MAN LIKES HIS PENNIES AND POUNDS.

LET YOUR WORLD GO AND UNDERSTAND JESUS CHRIST THEN A PART OF THE TRUTH AND GOD YOU WILL BE, LIKE JESUS YOU MUST HAVE THE FAITH TO LET GO OF YOUR WORLD THEN YOU WILL RECEIVE REAL FAITH BY MAKING THE SACRIFICE OF YOUR WORLD TO GOD.

WHEN MAN BECOMES WHAT HE IS NOT, THEN HE WILL BE AS HE IS, THEN WHEN HE IS, WHAT HE IS, THEN HE WILL NO LONGER BE, WHAT HE IS NOT, IF HE STAYS BEING WHAT HE IS, INSTEAD OF WHAT HE IS NOT, THEN HE WILL NOT BE, AS HE SHOULD BE, WHICH IS HOW HE IS NOT, THEN WHEN HE IS AS HE SHOULD BE, AND NOT AS HE IS NOT, THEN HE WILL NOT BE, AS HE SHOULD NOT BE, TO BE AS HE SHOULD BE, IS TO BE AS HE IS, BUT HE IS NOT, TO BE AS HE IS NOT, IS TO BE AS HE SHOULD BE, SO BE AS YOU SHOULD BE, BY NOT BEING AS YOU ARE NOT, THEN WE WILL ALL BE, AS WE SHOULD HAVE BEEN, BEFORE WE BECAME NOT, AS WE SHOULD BE, THEN WE WILL NOT BE, AS WE ARE NOT, AND BE AS WE ARE, THEN WE WILL TRULY BE, AS WE TRULY ARE, AND NOT, AS WE ARE NOT.

WHEN YOU THINK ABOUT SOMETHING, OR ABOUT HOW SOMETHING IS, THEN THINK, WHAT IT WAS BEFORE YOU THOUGHT ABOUT IT? BECAUSE WHEN YOU THINK ABOUT IT, IT STILL IS WHAT IT WAS BEFORE YOU STARTED THINKING ABOUT IT, THE THOUGHT OF IT, JUST CHANGES WHAT IT IS, IN THE MIND, BUT THE TRUTH IS, IS THAT IT STILL IS, WHAT IT IS, EVEN BEFORE YOU STARTED THE THOUGHT OF IT, THE FACT THAT YOU ARE THINKING ABOUT IT, DOES NOT TRULY CHANGE WHAT IT IS, AND TRULY WAS BEFORE YOU STARTED THINKING ABOUT IT, SO THINK TO YOURSELF, WHAT IS IT, BEFORE YOU START THINKING ABOUT IT, AND THEN YOU WILL KNOW WHAT IT TRULY WAS, WHICH IS WHAT IT IS, BEFORE YOU HAD THE THOUGHT ON WHAT IT WAS OR THINKING ABOUT IT, THEN ONCE YOU KNOW THE TRUTH OF IT, BEING WHAT IT WAS, AND WAS BEFORE YOU STARTED THINKING ABOUT WHAT IT IS AND WAS, YOU WILL THEN THINK OF IT, NO MORE AND JUST KNOW WHAT IT IS AND IS NOT, HENCE THE TRUTH SHALL PREVAIL AND IT WILL BE ALL WHAT IT IS WHICH IS

THE WAY IT SHOULD BE, IS THE WAY IT WAS, BEFORE IT CAME TO THE WAY IT SHOULD NOT, AND THE WAY FOR IT TO BE, IS NOT TO BE AS IT IS, BUT TO BE AS IT IS NOT, THEN WHEN IT IS NOT, THE WAY IT SHOULD BE, THEN IT WILL BE AS IT SHOULD BE, WHICH WAS HOW IT WAS, BEFORE WE THOUGHT HOW IT SHOULD BE, WHICH IS WHY IT IS NOT, RATHER THAN WHAT IT SHOULD BE, THEN WHEN IT IS WHAT IT WAS, THEN IT WILL NOT BE AS IT IS, BUT HOW IT IS NOT, BUT BY IT NOT BEING THE WAY IT WAS, MEANS WE WILL NOT KNOW HOW IT SHOULD BE, AND ALL WE WILL KNOW IS HOW IT IS, RATHER THAN HOW IT IS NOT, SO LET'S ALL TRY TO MAKE IT THE WAY IT WAS, AND SHOULD BE, RATHER THAN KEEPING IT THE WAY IT IS, WHICH IS HOW IT SHOULD NOT BE, WHICH MEANS IT SHOULD BE, AT THE END AS IT WAS, IN THE BEGINNING SO WE CAN SEE THE END OF HOW IT SHOULD NOT HAVE BEEN, AND LIVE TO OUR END OF HOW IT SHOULD BE.

IF A MAN THINKS HE KNOWS, THEN HE DOES NOT KNOW,

THEN IF YOU DO NOT KNOW, THEN WHY THINK YOU KNOW,

IF YOU THINK YOU KNOW, THEN YOU DO NOT KNOW,

UNTIL YOU KNOW, THEN YOU WILL KNOW,

WHEN YOU DO KNOW, AND YOU KNOW THAT YOU KNOW,

THEN YOU WILL TRULY KNOW, AND NOT HAVE TO THINK YOU KNOW,

BUT UNTIL YOU KNOW, AND KNOW THAT YOU KNOW, THEN YOU DO NOT KNOW IT,

BUT THEN WHEN YOU KNOW, AND KNOW IT, THEN YOU WILL NOT HAVE TO THINK

YOU KNOW IT, WHEN YOU DO NOT, WHEN YOU DO NOT KNOW,

KNOW THAT YOU DO NOT KNOW, AND KNOW IT, THEN YOU WILL KNOW,

BUT DO NOT THINK YOU KNOW, AND KNOW IT, THEN YOU WILL KNOW,

BUT DO NOT THINK YOU KNOW, WHEN YOU KNOW, YOU DO NOT,

TO KNOW YOU DO NOT KNOW, IS TO KNOW, SO KNOW IT,

THEN YOU WILL UNDERSTAND, WHAT YOU DO NOT KNOW, YOU KNOW,

AND WILL NOT THINK, AND WHAT YOU KNOW, AND KNOW IT,

YOU WILL SPEAK, OR SPEAK WITHOUT SPEAKING, BECAUSE YOU KNOW,

THEN YOU TRULY HAVE KNOWING, AND THE UNDERSTANDING OF WHAT IT IS TO KNOW.

WHILST YOU ARE IN THE WORLD START UNDERSTANDING YOURSELF SO YOU MAY THEN HAVE UNDERSTANDING OF THE WORLD TO BE UNDERSTANDING OF THE TRUTH WHICH IS TO UNDERSTAND GOD THEN TO BE PASSING ON THE UNDERSTANDING SO THAT THE NEXT GENERATION CAN BE GROWING UP WITH THE UNDERSTANDING SO THEY MAY EXIST BY THE UNDERSTANDING SO THERE MAY BE GRACEFUL PEACE AND CONTENTMENT ON EARTH BEING A PART OF GOD'S WORLD.......

HAVE LOVE SO YOU MAY GIVE IT
HAVE FAITH SO YOU MAY SHARE IT
HAVE CHARITY SO YOU MAY BE CHARITABLE
HAVE HOPE SO YOU MAY HOPE ALL WILL KNOW GOD
HAVE CONTENTMENT SO YOU MAY BE CONTENT
HAVE GRACE SO YOU MAY BE GRACEFUL
HAVE SELFLESSNESS SO YOU MAY BE SELFLESS
HAVE RESPECT SO YOU MAY GIVE IT
HAVE INNER STRENGTH SO YOU MAY KEEP IT FOR GOD

YOU HAVE THE MIND
TO TAKE THE KNOWLEDGE
TO HAVE THE THOUGHT
OF THE WORD UNDERSTAND
TO KNOW
THE TRUTH
OF GOD
WHICH IS THE EXISTENCE OF

IF MAN TRULY KNEW <u>GOD</u> THEN HE WOULD KNOW <u>NOTHING</u> GOD WOULD BE ABLE TO DO HIS WORK AND ALL WE WOULD SE AND KNOW WOULD BE THE <u>EXISTENCE</u>.

SO LONG AS THERE IS A WORLD WHERE PEOPLE THINK THEY KNOW THEN GOD CANNOT PREVAIL HENCE NO PEACE AND CONTENTMENT ON EARTH.

BECAUSE PEOPLE ONLY KNOW WHAT THEY HAVE BEEN TOLD BY OTHERS THEY HAVE TO COME TO THEIR OWN TRUTH BECAUSE THAT'S ALL THEY HAVE NOW. IF YOU GIVE UNTO THEM A BIT OF THE REAL TRUTH BECAUSE IT IS SO FAR AWAY FROM THE WORLD'S TRUTH THEY GET FRIGHTENED AND DEFENSIVE.

PEOPLE ARE OFTEN FRIGHTENED OF WHAT THEY CANNOT UNDERSTAND SO UNDERSTAND THEM.

IF YOU TRULY BECOME A PART OF GOD THEN YOU WILL BE OUT OF THE WORLD AND IN THE TRUTH BUT THEN YOU MUST TREAT THE WORLD YOU LEFT BEHIND WITH UNDERSTANDING AND GRACE BECAUSE THIS IS WHAT GOD DEMANDS.

REMEMBER PEOPLE IN THE WORLD DO NOT KNOW WHAT THEY ARE DOING SO DO NOT JUDGE THEM OR HOLD WITH YOU A BITTER TONGUE BECAUSE AS SOON AS YOU DO THIS YOU WILL HAVE TO BE THINKING AND AS SOON AS YOU DO THAT YOU WILL BE PULLED BACK IN THE WORLD AND LOSE YOUR UNDERSTANDING AND WILL NO LONGER BE WITH GOD.......

REMEMBER GOD REQUIRES YOUR WORLD
         REQUIRES YOUR PAST
         REQUIRES YOU'RE THINKING MIND
         SO THEN YOU HAVE NO WORLD NO
         PAST NO THINKING

REWARD   NO WEIGHT OF THE WORLD AN EMPTY
           MIND OF THINKING
           A WARM HEART UNDERSTANDING
           THOUGHTS OF UNDERSTANDING
           THE TRUTH A PART OF GOD'S WORLD

IF YOU DO THIS THEN YOU WILL HAVE SOLIDNESS
INSIDE YOU AND NO LONGER REQUIRE WHAT THE
HUMAN WORLD HAS TO OFFER.......

WHAT THIS IS SAYING TO YOU IS BE A PART OF IT THE
WORLD WITHOUT BEING A PART OF IT THEN IN YOU
WILL HAVE NOTHING TO DO WITH IT AND PEACE MAY
PREVAIL.......

If man thinks he knows, then he does not know, then if you do not know, then why think you know, if you think you know, then you do not know, until you know, then you will know, then you do know, and know that you know, and you will truly know, and not have to think you know, but until you know, and know that you know, then you do not know it. But then when you know, and know it, then you will not have to think you know it, when you do not, when you do not know, know that you do not know, and know it, then you will know, but do not think you know, when you know, you do not, to know you do not know, is to know, so know it, then you will understand, what you do not know, you know, and will not think, and what you know, and know it, you will speak, or speak without speaking, knowing, and the understanding of what it is to know.

SO YOU THINK THAT YOU'RE A HUMAN DO YOU WELL SO LONG AS YOU KEEP THINKING THAT THEN YOU WILL KEEP DOING WHAT HUMANS DO AND FEELING WHAT THE FEEL AND THINKING WHAT THEY THINK BUT LET ME TELL YOU THAT YOU ARE NOT HUMAN ONLY BECAUSE MAN HAS TOLD YOU THAT YOU ARE HUMAN SO YOU ARE EXPECTED TO DO HUMAN THING. BUT THE FACT IS THAT YOU ARE A PART OF THE UNIVERSE HENCE GOD AND YOU ARE NOT EXPECTED TO DO ANYTHING THAT YOU DO IN THE HUMAN WORLD OTHER THAN TO KNOW AND LOVE GOD. ONCE YOU TRULY KNOW GOD THEN YOU WILL KNOW THAT YOU ARE NOT HUMAN AT ALL, ALL YOU ARE IS A PART OF THE UNIVERSE A PART OF GOD BEING HUMAN IS WHAT MAKES LIFE AND THIS MAKES CHAOS IN THE MOST CHAOTIC WAY, HENCE WAR, HATE, FALSE LOVE, DESIRE WHAT WE THINK IS GOOD AND BAD AND DO NOT TRULY KNOW AND KNOW THAT E KNOW AND WHY ALL OF THIS YES BECAUSE WE THINK * * * * * SO IF YOU ARE WONDERING TO YOURSELF WHY DO PEOPLE DO WHAT THEY DO IT'S BECAUSE THEY THINK AS HUMANS THINK. WHEN WE CAN ALL STOP BEING HUMAN AND BE WHERE WE SHOULD BE THEN PEACE. BUT IF YOU KEEP ON THINKING THAT YOU ARE HUMAN THEN YOU WILL FEEL THAT YOU HAVE TO DO AS OTHER HUMANS DO AND SAY WHAT OTHER HUMANS SAY.

THE TROUBLE WITH YOU IS THAT YOU SAY HOW CAN THEY DO THIS? HOW CAN THEY DO THAT? HOW CAN THEY SAY THIS? HOW CAN THEY SAY THAT? I WOULD NOT DO THIS OR THAT. I WOULD NOT SAY THIS OR THAT. WELL THERE ARE A LOT OF THINGS THAT THEY WOULD NOT DO OR SAY THAT YOU DO OR SAY SO WHEN IS IT GOING TO END SWELL WHEN YOU STOP OPINIONISING ON WHAT YOU WOULD NOT DO OR SAY STOP JUDGING ON WHAT YOU THINK IS RIGHT OR WRONG AND STOP BEING A HUMAN BEING. THEN WE CAN GET ON WITH TRULY JUST UNDERSTANDING AND PEACE MAY PREVAIL.

YOU CAN START BY TEACHING YOUR CHILDREN ABOUT LOVE AND UNDERSTANDING NOT TAKING THEM TO THE SCHOOL OF THE WORLD BUT KEEP THEM AT HOME AND TEACH THEM OF GRACE, LOVE, PEACE, UNDERSTANDING SO WE MAY HAVE PEACE. ALL SCHOOLS DO IS GET THEM READY FOR THE WORLD OF CONFUSION INSTEAD OF LEARNING HOW TO BE CONTENT UNDERSTANDING AND BASICALLY SHOWING EXAMPLES OF GOD. SCHOOLS GET THEM READY FOR THE WORLDLY BATTLE WHICH NO ONE DESERVES IF YOU HAVE CHILDREN KEEP THEM FROM LEARNING THE WORLDLY SCHOOL THINGS AND WHEN THEY COME HOME TEACH OF LOVE AND UNDERSTANDING. THEN WHEN THEY GO TO SCHOOL IT WILL MEAN NOTHING TO THEM AND WHEN THEY COME HOME YOU WILL TECH THEM HOW TO BE CONTENT WITH THEIR LIFE, TRULY CONTENT.

YOU SEE THE WORLD BEING THE WAY IT IS NEEDS YOUR CHILDREN TO GO THERE TO HELP KEEP IT GOING THE WAY IT IS BUT IF THEY ARE LEARNING HOW TO BE PEACEFUL THEN WE WILL SEE REAL CHANGE FOR THE GOOD OF MANKIND BUT IF WE KEEP THE SYSTEM GOING THEN MORE CHAOS WILL FOLLOW HENCE NO PEACE ON EARTH.

THE WORLD IS NOTHING IT LEADS TO NOTHING AND THE RESULT OF IT IS NOTHING. NOW IF YOU COULD UNDERSTAND THE TRUE NOTHINGNESS OF IT ALL THEN YOU WOULD WANT NO MORE TO DO WITH IT SO UNDERSTAND THE NOTHINGNESS THEN AGAIN REAL CHANGE CAN START. REMEMBER TO GET TRUE PEACE AND UNDERSTANDING YOU MUST STOP THINKING AS I KNOW YOU CAN THEN YOU WILL FEEL THE CHANGE THAT WILL TAKE PLACE WITHIN YOU AND THEN YOU WILL UNDERSTAND THE RESULT WHICH WILL BE PEACE.

WHEN YOU STEP OUTSIDE IN THE AIR AND LOOK UP THAT IS REAL, AND WHEN YOU LOOK FORWARD AND SEE ANYTHING THAT IS COMPOSED BY THE ELEMENTS AND NOT BY MAN THAT IS REAL ALSO. BUT WE HAVE DECIDED TO CALL REALISM NAMES SO WE CAN SEE WHAT IS REAL BUT WITH THE UNREALISM OF NAMES THAT WE HAVE CHOSEN FOR THE NATURAL ELEMENTS. SO WE HAVE TURNED REALISM INTO UNREALISM WHICH MEANS THAT WE DO NOT SEE IT AS IT REALLY IS, BUT SEE IT AS WE KNOW IT TO BE BY THE NAME GIVEN TO IT BY THE THINKING MIND.

ANYTHING THAT IS NOT COMPOSED BY THE ELEMENTS (GOD) IS NOT REAL IT EXISTS BUT IT IS UNREALISM AND NOTHING. NOW ANYTHING COMPOSED BY THE ELEMENTS IS REAL IT EXISTS AND IS TRULY NOTHING, IT IS THE EXISTENCE OF NOTHING UNTIL YOU INVENT A NAME FOR IT WHICH TAKES ITS TRUE REALISM AWAY.

WHEN YOU SPEAK EVERYTHING YOU SAY IS NOT TRUE UNLESS IT IS OF UNDERSTANDING WHICH IS TRUTH, SO LOOSE CONVERSATION IS COMPILED WITH SOME TRUE WORDS BUT HAVE A MEANINGLESS TRUTH AND AN UNREAL UNDERSTANDING.

EXAMPLE, TWO PEOPLE TALKING IN THE UNREAL SENSE, "HELLO, IT WAS A LOVELY DAY TODAY. WHAT DID YOU THINK" REPLY "OH YES, IT WAS GREAT, I ENJOYED IT." NOW THERE IS NO SUCH WORD AS LOVELY IN THE REAL SENSE AND THERE ARE NO DELAYS, NOW BY ASKING WHAT DID YOU THINK MEANS YOU ARE NOT TOO SURE IF IT WAS ENJOYABLE OR NOT SO YOU NEED A BACKUP AND BY ASKING THE PERSON WHAT THEY THOUGHT OF THE DAY IS ACTUALLY TELLING THEM WHAT YOU THOUGHT OF IT SO THEY REPLY IN REPLY TO YOUR QUESTION. BUT IF THE OTHER PERSON SAYS "NO I DID NOT THINK IT WAS A NICE DAY" THEN YOU WILL AGREE BECAUSE YOU WAS A NOT SURE AND DID NOT KNOW HOW IT WAWA SIN THE FIRST PLACE AND THAT'S WHY YOU ASKED AND SAID WHAT YOU DID.

NOW THE REPLY THERE IS NO GREAT IN THE UNREAL SENSE BU THEE IS IN THE REAL SENSE AND ENJOYED ONLY EXISTS IN THE UNREAL SENSE BUT JOY EXISTS I N THE REAL SENSE, AND ALSO NOT IN THE UNREAL. NOW I ENJOYED IT OR THE DAY, WHICH MEANS THERE WAS A SPECIFIC THING HE ENJOYED. NOW BECAUSE HE HAS RECEIVED AN OPINION ALREADY ABOUT THE DAY FROM SOMEONE WHO HE WAS WITH MEANS THAT HEARING FROM HIS FRIEND THAT HE THOUGHT IT WAS A LOVELY DAY MAY ENCOURAGE HIM TO SAY WHAT HE DID ONLY BECAUSE HIS FRIEND THOUGHT SO. SO HE IS REPLYING TO THE REPLY THAT HE FEELS HE HAS TO GIVE, BUT IF THE REPLY IS "NO I DID NOT ENJOY THE DAY" THEN EITHER HE IS TELLING THE TRUTH IN A VERY UNTRUTHFUL WAY BECAUSE THERE IS NOTHING TO BE ENJOYED BUT HE WAS LOOKING FOR IT AND DID NOT FIND OR YOU MAY HAVE UPSET HIM. THAT'S WHY HE IS SAYING THAT, BUT THEN YOU MAY HAVE UPSET HIM ANYWAY AND WHEN HE GAVE YOU THE ANSWER, "I ENJOYED IT" HE COULD HAVE BEEN SAYING THAT SO HE DID NOT UPSET YOU SO THEN HE IS LYING AND IT GOES ON AND ON. NOW A CONVERSATION IN THE REAL SENSE WOULD HAVE BEEN "THANK YOU FR THE COMPANY" REPLY "THANK YOU." THAT IS WHEN THERE IS TRUE UNDERSTANDING OF THE NOTHINGNESS.......

Love – understanding

Grace – knowing – joy

Truth – nothing

Existence – God

Yes – no – knowledge

Faith – hope – you

Within – in – out

Have – now

Inner self – the – show

Peace – content – explain – when

Is – real – what – thank you

For – good – hello

Be – as – being

I – go – shall – to – how

Do – all – way – give – receiving

Let – your – thoughts – a

Keep – charity

The nothing that makes the existence is God, and the existe4nce of God is the nothingness that is produced. God creates the nothingness which produces the existence of nothing. The existence of nothing is the existence of God. The nothingness creates the nothing that shows the existence of God. God creates the existence of nothing, which is produced by the nothingness, which was made by the existence of God. The existence of the existence as the existence of nothing, and the nothingness, of the nothing is the creation of God. God creates the nothingness which produces nothing and the result is the existence of nothing, which is the existence of God.

WHEN YOU GIVE SOMETHING, WHEN YOU HAVE UNDERSTANDING OF THE NOTHINGNESS, THEN YOU WILL GIVE FROM YOUR CHARITY WITHOUT EVER EXPECTING BACK. BECAUSE YOU UNDERSTAND THE UNREALISM OF THINGS, AND THAT WHEN YOU GIVE A THING, YOU ARE ACTUALLY GIVING ANY AT ALL TO THEM THAT THEY WILL TRULY HAVE, HENCE YOU WILL WANT FOR NOTHING IN RETURN BECAUSE YOU UNDERSTAND YOURSELF AND GIVE WHAT YOU HAVE BECAUSE YOU UNDERSTAND OTHERS. ALSO YOUR CHARITY OF GIVING WILL BE YOUR UNDERSTANDING OF OTHERS AS THEY ARE, AND KNOWING THAT IF THEY TAKE A SEED, YOU HAVE TRULY GIVEN THEM SOMETHING OF WHICH THEY WILL TRULY KEEP, AND KNOW THAT IF THEY TAKE IT, AND UNDERSTAND IT, THEN IN RETURN THEY HAVE GIVEN YOU UNDERSTANDING, BUT IF THEY DO NOT TAKE IT THEN YOU WILL HAVE UNDERSTANDING OF THAT.

WHEN YOU HAVE FAITH THEN YOU DO WHAT YOU DO FROM THE UNDERSTANDING OF THE FAITH, HENCE YOU ARE ABLE TO PASS IT ONTO OTHERS THROUGH YOUR ACTIONS OF UNDERSTANDING. WHATEVER INSTITUTION YOU ARE IN, WITH YOUR UNDERSTANDING YOU WILL BE ABLE TO DO BY YOUR FAITH WHICH YOU UNDERSTAND. YOUR FAITH AND UNDERSTANDING WILL BE YOUR GRACEFULNESS, WHICH COMES FROM YOUR FAITH THEN WHEN PEOPLE WANT TO UNDERSTAND, YOU HAVE THE FAITH TO SPEAK ONLY THE TRUTH.

WHEN YOU HAVE HOPE, THEN YOU HOPE ALL WILL KNOW GOD, AND THAT THOSE WHO DO NOT KNOW GOD AND YOU KNOW IT THROUGH THEIR ACTIONS OF THE WORLD, THEN YOU WILL NOT JUDGE THEM OR HOLD A BITTER TONGUE, BUT JUST HOPE THEY WILL KNOW GOD BECAUSE YOU UNDERSTAND.

THE EXISTENCE OF WHAT IS, IS BY THE EXISTENCE OF GOD.

THAT THAT IS NOT BY THE EXISTENCE OF GOD, AND HAS THE THINKING OF, IS NOT. THE EXISTENCE OF NOTHING THAT IS, BY THE EXISTENCE OF GOD, AND THAT THAT IS NOTHING, AND THOUGHT OF AS SOMETHING IS NOT.

THE EXISTENCE OF NOTHING IS GOD, BUT THE EXISTENCE OF GOD AS SOMETHING IS NOT. THE EXISTENCE OF THE EXISTENCE IS, BUT THE EXISTENCE OF SOMETHING IS NOT.

LISTEN AND LISTEN CAREFULLY ALL YOU HAVE TO DO IS STOP THINKING. IT IS A PHYSICAL EXERCISE, TAKE DEEP BREATHS, SQUINT YOUR EYES, YOU WILL FIND A WAY TO BLOCK OUT YOUR THINKING. THEN, AFTER A WHILE WHEN YOU COME TO REALISE THAT YOUR THINKING OF WORRY, ANGER, JEALOUSY IS ALL IN THE MIND AND CAN BE GOT RID OF BY NOT THINKING, THEN YOU WILL BEGIN NOT RELATING TO THEM BECAUSE THEY DO NOT EXIST UNLESS YOU HOLD ONTO THEM. HENCE YOUR OWN THOUGHTS WILL BEGIN TO MEAN NOTHING TO YOU THEN WHAT THE WORLD TAUGHT YOU WILL GO, HENCE YOU WILL LEAN THE OTHER WAY OF BEING AND PEACE WILL SET IN.

AFTER THAT PROGRESS WHATEVER COMES INTO YOUR MIND, EXAMPLE SUBCONSCIOUS THOUGHTS, MAYBE OF DESIRE YOU HAVE ALWAYS HAD FOR SOMETHING, OR MAYBE SOMETHING FROM THE PAST THAT HAS ALWAYS UPSET YOU BECAUSE YOU WAS UNABLE TO UNDERSTAND IT. NOW TO HAVE A MIND FREE FROM THE WORLD MEANS THAT YOU WILL BEGIN TO UNDERSTAND ALL YOUR SUBCONSCIOUS THOUGHTS INSTEAD OF ASKING WHAT THIS OR WHY THAT OR HOLDING RESENTMENTS, HENCE THEN YOU WILL HAVE NO FEELING ABOUT THEM BECAUSE THEY HAVE BEEN UNDERSTOOD WHICH IS WHAT THEY WERE LOOKING FOR IN THE FIRST PLACE, ALAS, THEY WILL MEAN NOTHING TO YOU ANYMORE AND THEY WILL GO. HENCE YOU WILL BE FREE.

YOU MUST KEEP WORKING ALL THE TIME KEEPING THE WORLDLY THOUGHTS AT BAY AND UNDERSTANDING ANY SUBCONSCIOUS THOUGHTS, HENCE KEEPING A CLEAR MIND HENCE PEACE AND CONTENTMENT WITHIN YOU.

UNDERSTANDING IN THEE END IS ALL YOU WILL BE LEFT WITH, YOU WILL NOT JUDGE ANYONE AS GOOD OR BAD BECAUSE YOU WILL UNDERSTAND THEM. YOU WILL BECOME GRACEFUL WITH YOUR UNDERSTANDING,

AND YOU WILL NOT HAVE THE NEED TO DO MANY OF THE THINGS YOU DO NOW BECAUSE YOU WILL UNDERSTAND THE NOTHINGNESS OF IT ALL.

IF YOU DO NOT THINK OF ANYTHING GAS YOU THINK IT IS THE TRUTH IS THAT IT'S NOTHING, THE TRUE MEANING OF THE WORD, IT IS ONLY SOMETHING IF YOU THINK IT IS SOMETHING THAT IS WHY THERE IS NO TRUTH IN THE WORLD, BECAUSE EVERYTHING IS ONLY WHAT PEOPLE THINK IT IS, BUT IF YOU DO NOT THINK THEN YOU WILL UNDERSTAND TRULY THAT IT IS NOTHING.

UNLOAD ALL THAT THE WORLD HAS TAUGHT YOU AND STEP INTO THE REAL SIDE OF EXISTENCE, THERE IS ONLY PEACE AND LOVE OF UNDERSTANDING, CONTENTMENT, GRACE AND GOD. ALL WONDERS OF THE UNIVERSE AND EVERYTHING WILL BE OPENED UP TO YOU IF YOU JUST LET YOUR MADE UP SELF GO AND BECOME YOUR REAL SELF WHICH HAS NO SELF, THEN YOU WILL BE A PART OF UNDERSTANDING AND TRUE KNOWING RATHER THAN A PART OF THE GAME MAN HAS PLAYED AND DECEIVED HIMSELF WITH FOR SO LONG.

IT'S CALLED IN RELATIVE TERMS NOT BEING HUMAN AND INSTEAD BEING A PART OF THE UNIVERSE WHICH YOU REALLY ARE AND A PART OF THE UNDERSTANDING WHICH MAKES IT.

START FINDING PEACE IN YOURSELF NOW SO THAT OTHERS CAN PICK UP THE SEED OF PEACE. IF YOU FIND PEACE AND CONTENTMENT WITHIN THEN YOU WILL CHANGE AND THE NEXT PERSON CAN NOTICE IT AND WONDER TO THEMSELVES WHAT HAVE YOU GOT THAT THEY HAVE NOT, AND THIS WILL BE PEACE AND CONTENTMENT WITHIN. NOW UNLESS YOU START TO CHANGE THEN THERE WILL BE NO CHANGE FOR THE GOD OF YOURSELF OF MANKIND AND THINGS WILL JUST GO ON IN THE FASHION THAT THEY HAVE BEEN AND YOU MUST ADMIT IT'S NOT TOO GOOD FOR YOU IS IT? NO, WELL THEN CHANGE FOR THE BETTER. START FINDING UNDERSTANDING FOR OTHERS AND YOURSELF INSTEAD OF MAKING JUDGMENTS ABOUT PEOPLE AND THINGS AND GIVE UP YOUR OPINIONS SO THE NEXT PERSON CAN LEARN A DIFFERENT WAY OF BEING OTHER THAN WHAT THE WORLD HAS TAUGHT THEM.

AT THE MOMENT EVERYTHING IS IN CHAOS. YOU LOSE YOUR TEMPER YOU ARE IMPATIENT BASICALLY, YOU ARE HUMAN AND SO LONG AS YOU CONTINUE TO BE HUMAN THEN EVERYONE ELSE WILL CONTINUE TO BE, HENCE NO PEACE FOR YOU. SO FIND YOU'RE INNER PEACE SO YOU MAY PLANT THE SEED FOR THE NEXT PERSON AND THEN PEOPLE WILL BEGIN TO BE MORE CONTENT WITHIN THEMSELVES AND STOP SEEKING WHAT THE WORLD HAS TO OFFER WHICH BASICALLY IS CONFUSION AND CHAOS.

IT IS UP TO YOU TO MAKE THE REAL CHANGE BY FIRST MAKING THE CHANGE IN YOURSELF THEN IT CAN BE SPREAD AND WHO KNOWS BUT GOD MAYBE UTOPIA, BUT YOU HAVE GOT TO MAKE THE SACRIFICE FOR YOURSELF SO YOU CAN BE CONTENTFUL AND PEACEFUL THEN OTHERS CAN SEE AND LEARN BY YOU BUT YOU MUST MAKE THE FIRST STEPS THEN THE REST WILL COME.

YOU KNOW SOMETHING AND KNOW THAT YOU KNOW IS SOMETHING YOU WILL NEVER HAVE UNLESS YOU STOP THINKING AND COME OUT FROM THE WORLD. THE WORLD THAT YOU HAVE BEEN A PART OF, LET'S FACE IT, WHAT HAVE YOU GOT REALLY GOD SO IT CAN NEVER BE TAKEN AWAY BY ANYBODY OR ANYTHING, *WELL* EXACTLY YOU HAVE NOTHING NOW FIND SOMETHING WITHIN YOUR TRUE SELF AND THAT WILL NEVER BE ABLE TO BE TAKEN AWAY. WHAT IS THAT YOU TRULY HAVE WITHIN YOU, YOUR TRUE SELF, IT IS TRUE LOVE TRUE UNDERSTANDING TRUE PEACE AND CONTENTMENT AND A WARM HEART, BUT TO GET THIS FROM WITHIN YOURSELF YOU MUST GIVE UP ALL THAT THE WORLD TAUGHT YOU AND ALL YOU TOOK FROM IT THEN TRUE PEACE MAY PREVAIL FOR YOU AND MANKIND.

I KNOW THAT YOU HAVE THAT STRONG FEELING TO LIVE A LIFE AND BE PART OF IT THAT'S ONLY BECAUSE YOU ARE SCARED AND FEEL THAT YOU ARE HERE FOR A WORLDLY PURPOSE AND THAT YOU ARE LOSING OUT ON SOMETHING BUT UNDERSTAND AND TRULY UNDERSTAND THE NOTHINGNESS OF IT ALL THEN YOU WILL KNOW AND TRULY KNOW THAT YOU KNOW THAT THE WORLD IS NOT WORTH PLAYING WITH ANYMORE HENCE YOU MAY FIND PEACE WITHIN.

ALL THE WORLD HAS GIVEN YOU IS HOW TO PLAY THE PART, IT TAKES YOU UP IN WHAT YOU THINK IS HAPPINESS ONE MINUTE AND DOWN IN UNHAPPINESS THE NEXT SO ALL THE TIME YOU ARE GOING UP AND DOWN UP AND DOWN GOING NOWHERE LEARNING NOTHING OF ANY TRUE VALUE TO YOURSELF OR ANYBODY ELSE HENCE DECEIT AND CONFUSION. NOW UNDERSTAND THE TRUE NOTHINGNESS OF IT ALL (THE WORLD) THEN YOU CAN FIND PLENTY OF TIME FINDING YOUR TRUE SELF, WHICH HAS NOTHING TO DO WITH THE WORLD THAT HUMANS HAVE INVENTED FOR HIS OWN PLAYGROUND.

SO JUST DO WHAT YOU HAVE TO DO TO BE HERE ON EARTH WHICH IS EAT AND DRINK WATER AND REPRODUCE THAT'S AL YOU TRULY HAVE TO DO, ANYTHING ELSE THAT YOU THINK YOU HAVE TO DO WITHOUT KNOWING TRULY THAT YOU HAVE TO DO IT, MEANS THAT YOU DO NOT HAVE TO DO IT ALL SO GIVE IT UP THEN PEACE MAY PREVAIL.......

ANYTHING YOU ARE WANTING OR FEEL THAT YOU NEED FROM THE WORLD IS JUST HELPING IT TO CONTINUE IN THE WAY THAT IT IS SO IF YOU GIVE UP YOUR DESIRES FORM THE WORLD THEN SOME PROGRESS CAN START IN A DIFFERENT WAY OF BEING. YOU SEE YOU ARE NOT CONTENT ENOUGH TO SIT AT HOME AND DO NOTHING UNTIL SOMETHING HAS TO BE DONE. INSTEAD YOU GO LOOKING FOR THINGS TO DO HENCE KEEPING IT ALL GOING.

YOU CANNOT HAVE PEACE BY WANTING THE WORLD TO BE PEACEFUL YOU MUST FIND IT WITHIN YOURSELF WHICH MEANS MAKING SACRIFICES FOR YOURSELF LIKE STOP THINKING THEN ONCE YOU FIND INNER PEACE THEN YOUR ACTIONS WILL CHANGE NOTHING WILL GET TO YOU, YOU WILL BE A PEACEFUL PERSON THEN BY YOUR ACTIONS OF PEACE OTHER PEOPLE WILL NOTICE AND TAKE THE SEED FROM YOU HENCE PEASE WILL BE PASSED ON IN A TRULY PEACEFUL WAY BUT SO LONG AS YOU ARE PROTESTING ABOUT THIS ABOUT THAT THEN HOW CAN PEACE AND UNDERSTANDING BE SHOWN.......

LET'S FACE IT HOW WOULD YOU TRULY LIKE NEVER TO HAVE ANYMORE HANG-UPS OR PROBLEMS AGAIN WELL YOU CAN DO THIS DO NOT LOOK FOR HAPPINESS ANYMORE BECAUSE YOU KNOW IT CAN BE TAKEN AWAY AND THEN YOU WOULD HAVE SADNESS SO WHAT DO YOU DO FIND PEACE AND CONTENTMENT WITHIN YOURSELF THEN YOU WILL BE IN THE MIDDLE WHICH IS NOTHING. DO NOT WANT FOR ANYTHING THEN YOU WILL

NEVER BE SHORT HENCE NO FRUSTRATION. SO YOU GIVE UP ONE THING THEN ANOTHER THEN ANOTHER KEEP MAKING THE FIRST STEPS FOR YOURSELF THEN THE REST WILL FOLLOW. SO REMEMBER IF YOU DO NOT GIVE UP YOUR WANTS BECAUSE IT DOES THIS FOR YOU

AND IF YOU DO NOT GIVE UP YOUR NOT WANTING BECAUSE IT DOES NOT DO THAT FOR YOU THEN FOR YOU NO PEACE AND CONTENTMENT.......

AFTER ALL JUST LOOK AT YOURSELF YOU ARE NO MORE THAN A CHILD WHO THINKS HE IS IN A PLAYGROUND PLAYING GAMES AND NOT TRULY KNOWING OR LEARNING ANYTHING OTHER THAN TO PLAY GAMES NOW GET RID OF ALL THAT THE WORLD HAS TAUGHT YOU AND START AGAIN. THIS TIME WITH TRUE UNDERSTANDING WHICH YOU WILL FIND WITHIN THE PEACE AND CONTENTMENT WITHIN YOU WHICH YOU HAVE BUT YOU MUST GIVE UP YOUR THINKING OF THE WORLD AND THINK OF IT NO MORE AND THEN BEGIN TO UNDERSTAND AND YOU WILL MAKE FALSE JUDGEMENTS NO MORE JUST UNDERSTANDING.......

DO YOU FEEL THAT YOU HAVE HAD ENOUGH OF THE WORLD AND ALL THE PRESSURES YOU HAVE PICKED UP FROM IT.......

WELL LET ME TELL YOU SOMETHING NOW IS A CHANCE FOR YOU TO GIVE UP ALL YOUR WORLDLY THINGS THAT YOU THINK MAKE YOU HAPPY AND NOW FIND CONTENTMENT WITHIN YOURSELF.

LET ME START BY TELLING YOU THAT THE WORLD IS A STAGE, YES AND LIKE A STAGE IT'S ALL MADE UP (NOT REAL FALSE) THEREFORE ANYTHING THE WORLD GIVES YOU IS NOT REAL AND TRUE BECAUSE IT CAN BE TAKEN AWAY. SO ANYTHING YOU DO THAT YOU THINK MAKES YOU HAPPY WHAT HAPPENS WHEN THAT IS TAKEN AWAY? *WELL* YES THAT'S RIGHT YOU BECOME UNHAPPY AND THEN YOUR MIND STARTS THINKING OH NO NOW WHAT AM I GOING TO DO? SO YOUR MIND THINKS AND LOOKS FOR ANOTHER WORLDLY THING WHATEVER IT IS TO PUT YOU BACK AGAIN IN HAPPINESS OF WHAT YOU THINK IS GOING TO MAKE YOU CONTENT.

NOW REMEMBER ANY OPINIONS OR JUDGEMENTS YOU HAVE ABOUT ANYTHING IS NOT TRUE. WHY FOR EXAMPLE IF YOU THINK THAT SOMEONE IS AN IDIOT SO YOU THINK THEIR AN IDIOT THEN SOMEONE ELSE THINKS THAT THEY'RE CLEVER THEN YOU HAVE JUST TWO OPINIONS ON WHAT THIS SOMEONE IS NOW WHAT IS HE TRULY WITHOUT ANY OF YOUR JUDGEMENTS? WHAT TRULY IS HE?

ALL WORLDLY PROBLEMS WITH PEOPLE AND THE WORLD IS THAT EVERYBODY LIES YES AND YOU CAN SAY THINGS AND DO THINGS THAT YOU DO NOT KNOW WHAT YOU ARE DOING AND YOU CAN FIND NO ROOM IN YOUR HEARTS FOR UNDERSTANDING ALL YOU CAN DO IS MAKE JUDGEMENTS THAT SUIT YOUR SELF INTEREST. WHAT A SHAME.

NOW GIVE IT ALL UP SO THAT PEACE MAY BE GIVEN A REAL CHANCE TO PREVAIL BECAUSE AFTER ALL IF YOU DO NOT FIND REAL PEACE WITHIN YOURSELF AND MAKE THE FIRST STEP THEN HOW CAN OTHERS PICK UP THE SEED SO YOU MAKE THE SACRIFICE, GIVE UP YOUR TINY DECEITFUL WORLD AND FIND THE TRUTH THEN THE NEXT PERSON CAN PICK SOMETHING SOLID UP FROM YOU INSTEAD OF THE WORLDLY NONSENSE THAT YOU ARE CONSTANTLY PASSING ON.

AND ALL YOU HAVE TO DO IS STOP THINKING, YES STOP THINKING, GIVE YOUR MIND A CHANCE TO WORK AS IT REALLY SHOULD AND NOT AS YOU HAVE AS THE WORLD HAS MADE IT THEN PEACE AND CONTENTMENT FOR YOU SHALL BEGIN ITS COURSE.......

Milton Keynes UK
Ingram Content Group UK Ltd.
UKHW031840161024
449753UK00001B/46